Other McGraw-Hill Books of Interest

BAKER • *Downsizing*
BAKER • *Networking the Enterprise*
BATES • *Disaster Recovery for LANs*
BOAR • *Implementing Client/Server Computing*
BUNZEL and MORRIS • *Multimedia Applications Development*
DERN • *The Internet Guide for New Users*
DEWIRE • *Client/Server Computing*
GRAY • *Open Systems and IBM*
IBM • *IBM Dictionary of Computing*
KEYES • *Software Engineering Productivity Handbook*
LARIJANI • *The Virtual Reality Primer*
LYON and GLUCKSON • *MIS Manager's Appraisal Guide*
ROTHSTEIN • *Ace the Technical Interview*
STERN • *Preventing Computer Fraud*
SIMON • *How to Be a Successful Computer Consultant*
SIMON • *The Computer Professional's Survival Guide*
SIMON • *The Computer Professional's Guide to Effective Communications*
SIMON • *Downsized But Not Out*
RANADE • *The Best of BYTE*
TERPLAN • *Effective Management of Local Area Networks*
DEWIRE • *Text Management*

To order or receive additional information on these or any other McGraw-Hill titles, please call 1-800-822-8158 in the United States. In other countries, contact your local McGraw-Hill representative.

BC14BCZ

How to Be a Successful Systems Manager in a PC Environment

Katherine H. Emery

McGraw-Hill, Inc.
New York San Francisco Washington, D.C. Auckland Bogotá
Caracas Lisbon London Madrid Mexico City Milan
Montreal New Delhi San Juan Singapore
Sydney Tokyo Toronto

Library of Congress Cataloging-in-Publication Data

Emery, Katherine H.
    How to be a successful systems manager in a PC environment /
Katherine H. Emery.
      p.   cm.
    Includes index.
    ISBN 0-07-019639-7 (h)—ISBN 0-07-019640-0 (p)
    1. Microcomputers. 2. Management information systems. I. Title.
QA76.5.E5623 1994
004.16′068—dc20   94–21801
                                                                                                     CIP

Copyright © 1995 by McGraw-Hill, Inc. All rights reserved. Printed in the United States of America. Except as permitted under the United States Copyright Act of 1976, no part of this publication may be reproduced or distributed in any form or by any means, or stored in a database or retrieval system, without the prior written permission of the publisher.

2 3 4 5 6 7 8 9 0 DOHDOH 9 0 9 8 7 6 5 4

ISBN 0-07-019640-0 P

The sponsoring editor for this book was Marjorie Spencer, the editing supervisor was Joseph Bertuna, and the production supervisor was Pamela A. Pelton. It was set in Century Schoolbook by Carol Woolverton Studio, Lexington, Massachusetts, in cooperation with Warren Publishing Services, Biddeford, Maine.

Printed and bound by R. R. Donnelley & Sons Company.

This book is printed on recycled, acid-free paper containing a minimum of 50% recycled de-inked fiber.

Information contained in this work has been obtained by McGraw-Hill, Inc., from sources believed to be reliable. However, neither McGraw-Hill nor its authors guarantees the accuracy or completeness of any information published herein and neither McGraw-Hill nor its authors shall be responsible for any errors, omissions, or damages arising out of use of this information. This work is published with the understanding that McGraw-Hill and its authors are supplying information, but are not attempting to render engineering or other professional services. If such services are required, the assistance of an appropriate professional should be sought.

To EHE
For inspiration, faith, and hope

Also
Everyone at S-O-F-T Industries for their assistance
&
SES for patience and support

Contents

Preface xv

Introduction: Hiring a Systems Manager—A Note to the Boss 1

   How About Mary, Our Resident Guru? 1
   Help Wanted 2
   The Ad 2
   The Application 3
   The Interview 6
   Orientation 9

Part 1 Taking Stock 11

Chapter 1. Your Mission 13

   Past Is Prologue—The History of Information Systems 13
   You and IS, or You Is IS 15
   What Your Job Is and What It Is Not 18
   Four Prime Objectives 18
   Don't Grab the Tiger Yet 19
   The Mission Statement 20
   The Action Plans 21
   To Do 23

Chapter 2. Getting Organized 25

   Ready, Set . . . 25
   Tao of Systems Management 26
   The Systems Profile 26
   The Master Planner 27
   The Project Folder 28
   The Workstation Folder 32
   To Do 34

Chapter 3. Working Through Committees — 35

- Your Nemesis, Your Salvation — 35
- Committee Etiquette — 35
- The Security Committee — 38
- The Planning Committee — 39
- Areas of Expertise — 42
- To Do — 43

Part 2 Taking Charge — 45

Chapter 4. Taking Inventory — 47

- Where to Begin — 47
- Skills Inventory — 48
- Hardware Inventory — 48
- Your First Preventive Maintenance Checkup — 52
- Keeping Track of It All — 54
- Commercial Software Inventory — 55
- Application Inventory — 57
- Mapping Your Terrain — 58
- To Do — 59

Chapter 5. Criticality Analysis — 61

- Lady Bug — 61
- Systems List — 62
- First Meeting of the Security Committee — 62
- Accessibility — 63
- Sensitivity — 64
- Integrity — 64
- Strategic Links — 64
- Backup Policies and Procedures — 65
- To Do — 66

Chapter 6. Disaster Planning — 67

- A Time to Act — 67
- The Bigger Picture — 68
- Working with Systems — 70
- Off-Site Backups — 70
- The Call — 71
- Audit Procedures — 71
- Insurance Coverage — 72
- To Do — 73

Contents   ix

Part 3   The Protective Audits   75

Chapter 7. Backup Audits   77

- Pay Now or Pay Later   77
- File Types   78
- Logs and Tools   79
- When, What, and Where   81
- The Restoration Process   84
- Testing . . . Testing . . .   86
  - Whoops: the accidentally deleted file   87
  - Damned spot: damaged areas on the disk   88
  - Something is rotten: data corruption   88
  - A funny thing happened: datapath failure   89
  - Crash: media failure   89
- Full Disk Recovery   89
  - The element of surprise   91
  - The results   91
- To Do   92

Chapter 8. Viral Protection   93

- The Big Scare   93
- Strains of Malignant Software   94
- Defensive Policies and Procedures   95
- In the Event of an Attack   96
- To Do   98

Chapter 9. Legal Audits   99

- Piracy   99
- The Initial Audit   101
- The Audit Report   103
- Custom Software   104
  - Viral infections   105
  - Service contracts   105
- Fraud   106
- Unauthorized Access   106
- Legal Issues Subcommittee   107
- To Do   107

Chapter 10. Access Audits   109

- Motives   109
- Solutions   111
- Systems Security Analysis   113
- Standard Security Precautions   115
- To Do   116

Chapter 11. Preventive Maintenance — 117

- Purpose — 117
- Internal Tasks — 117
- Disk Hardware Maintenance — 120
- Power PM — 120
- External Once-Over — 123
- To Do — 124

Chapter 12. Source Code Audits — 125

- Purpose — 125
- Where to Find Custom Applications — 125
- Security Ratings — 127
- Development Tools and Documentation — 127
- Input/Output and Testing Methods — 128
- Backup Security — 128
- Revision Management — 129
  - User comments — 130
  - Follow-up — 130
- Modified Commercial Software — 130
- To Do — 131

Part 4 Support Issues — 133

Chapter 13. Help Desk — 135

- Objectives — 135
- Skills and Attitudes — 137
  - The can-do approach — 137
  - Listening skills — 138
  - Follow-through — 140
- Call Management — 140
- Going Beyond the Call — 143
- To Do — 144

Chapter 14. Training — 145

- Training Philosophies — 145
- Training Triggers — 147
- Overcoming Barriers to Learning — 148
- Training Formats — 149
- Training the Trainers — 150
- To Do — 151

Chapter 15. Special Skills Development — 153

- Executive Training — 153
- Secretarial Training — 155
- The Word-Processing Users Group — 156
- To Do — 159

Chapter 16. News — 161

- Communicate! — 161
- Edit for Success — 162
- All the News — 163
- Scheduling — 164
- Survey Your Readers — 165
- To Do — 166

Part 5   Performance Issues — 167

Chapter 17. Hard-Disk Maintenance — 169

- Conventions — 169
- Disk Audit Procedures — 171
  - Internal checks — 172
  - External review — 173
  - The hard drive — 174
- To Do — 177

Chapter 18. The Basics — 179

- The Three R's — 179
- Document Management — 179
  - Chaos theory — 179
  - Document analysis — 180
  - Document management options — 183
- Spreadsheets — 184
  - Look for the clues — 185
  - Reel them in — 185
  - Coaching — 186
  - Checking the spreadsheet — 187
  - The Medusan spreadsheet — 187
  - Jack and the spreadsheet — 187
- Database Focus — 187
  - Tracking the database application — 188
  - Taming the wild database — 188
- To Do — 189

Chapter 19. Departmental Focus — 191

- Three Blind Men — 191
- Initial Meeting — 192
- Time Study Analysis — 192
- Results and Recommendations — 197
- Follow-up — 198
- To Do — 198

Chapter 20. Communications Focus — 201

- The Communications Map — 201
- The Ladder of Communication — 203

Wide Area Direct Connection Alternatives — 203
Application of New Technologies — 204
Departmental Recommendation — 205
To Do — 205

Part 6 Strategic Issues — 207

Chapter 21. New Technology Review — 209

Catching the Wave — 209
The New Technology Subcommittee — 210
New Technology Proposal — 211
New Technology Evaluation — 212
Education — 215
Product Evaluation and Selection — 216
Implementation — 217
When New Technology Eliminates Jobs — 217
To Do — 218

Chapter 22. Setting Standards — 219

The Needs of the Many — 219
The Pros — 219
The Cons — 220
The Ideal Candidate — 220
Justification — 220
The Task Force — 221
Eliminating Noncontenders — 222
May the Best Product Prevail — 223
Implementation — 224
To Do — 226

Chapter 23. Focus Studies — 227

The Goal Statement — 227
Information Gathering — 228
Option Evaluation — 229
Examples — 230
To Do — 231

Chapter 24. Strategic Planning — 233

The Year in Review, the Years Ahead — 233
Trickle-Down Planning — 235
Action Plans — 235
Budget and Schedule — 236
Improvement Plans — 236
To Do — 241

Appendix A. PC Management Tools 243

Appendix B. Manufacturer and Product List 255

Bibliography 263
Index 265

Preface

Have you been plagued with Automation Insomnia? Do you lie awake at night with weighty questions on the mind? Questions pertaining to the tremendous investment that has been made in equipment and software and data being stored and moved and manipulated on office microcomputers for which you have been made responsible? Certain nights these nagging and vaguely accusing questions might be centered around the relative safety of this massive investment. Is it safe? What might happen if . . . ? And then what would happen? Could it happen? Other nights perhaps the questions take a different but equally unsettling tack: Are we doing all we could be doing with this technology? Are we getting the most from our investment? What are our competitors doing with their computers? Questions like so many sheep, each turning to look at you, bleating "baaaaah" before leaping the fence.

If it helps, keep in mind that you are not alone. Microcomputer usage is on the rise, and so naturally are these types of questions. If you or someone you know is experiencing Automation Insomnia, take heart: This book was written for you.

You should also know that you are in relatively uncharted territory. While mainframe and minicomputer shops have always recognized the need for a systems manager, it is a new concept in the microcomputer world. The reason lies in the original functions allocated to the micrcomputer. While the big computers did the "important" work, the new microcomputers were seen as toys by comparison, used for small, insignificant tasks. In the early days many a microcomputer slipped in through the back door of business organizations under the label of office supplies and other creative account headings, diffusing the overall value of the combined investment in hardware and software (not to mention the data stored therein).

But times have changed and increasing numbers of mission-critical tasks are being done on these small but powerful engines. Over time these changes have added up so that today, taken in aggregate, the corporate microcomputer systems often outweigh the old mainframe in might and value. Further, the fact that this new asset is physically spread throughout the organization makes it all the more important to apply sound management techniques to this valuable and expanding resource.

Some of the old mainframe systems management policies and procedures can be applied, but in many respects it's a whole new game and the old rules are obsolete. In the mainframe world, control was the primary goal. The security and integrity of the system were your primary responsibility as mainframe systems manager. They remain important concerns, but certainly not your only ones today. The microcomputer, as already noted, is a widely distributed asset. Contrast this with the specially designed, raised-floor, temperature-controlled, dust-free, closed-door environment of the huge beasts of yore, and you begin to see a basic evolutionary change. The mainframe is a central repository; the microcomputer represents a drastic shift in the industry's inclination toward distributed processing. This makes information access much easier, and control much more difficult. It also results in many new security and integrity issues, and calls for creative and thoughtful strategic planning.

It is no longer possible for you as the systems manager to control who gets what information when. You can no longer ensure integrity and security by simply locking the door. Now your job will require the development of complex policies and procedures to protect the corporate data, while still ensuring quick, easy, and reliable access to information by those who need to know. And while the systems manager of old was the sole source of any new information flow, your job is to enable others to gather their own information.

These evolutionary developments are the impetus for this book. Its aim is to help you get started in your job as protector and provider, putting the nagging, nocturnal questions to rest, and putting the people you work for at ease, knowing you'll make sure information is secure yet accessible. That is your job as the microcomputer manager.

This book is meant to be used as a working guide. Read it over first to discover the full scope of your mission, and then go back and take it one chapter at a time. Use it to help acquire the information you need in order to protect and maximize the productivity of the incredible asset known as the corporate microcomputer. Also, use it as a reference guide. Keep it handy and make use of the schedules, sample forms, and checklists. Use it to work toward becoming a top-flight systems manager.

This book will help you establish goals, an approach, appropriate schedules for routine tasks, and methods to employ in order to accomplish your goals. You will learn that there are many creative aspects of your job which cannot be delineated in a simple checklist or policy statement. What this book attempts to do, more than dictate any one method, is to give you forms and checklists to consider, and otherwise to discuss possible approaches from which you can devise a plan most appropriate for your unique situation.

The Introduction to the book looks at your job from your boss's point of view. It is designed to help you (and your boss) understand the ideal attributes of a systems manager.

The first part of the book, Taking Stock, deals with setting up shop. You will learn more about the tasks ahead, and what you can hope to accomplish, how to get organized for maximum efficiency, and how to get the information you need about your environment fast. The next part, Taking Charge, covers those tasks which you must undertake first and fast: taking inventory so you know your terrain; doing a criticality analysis so you have a sense of what systems are most vital to the organization; and planning for disasters, which begins with immediate intervention and follows through with multiple levels of planning depending on the nature of the systems you have already uncovered.

The remaining four parts of the book divide systems management into four basic functions: Protective Audits, Support Issues, Performance Issues, and Strategic Issues.

Let's look at each part in greater detail.

Part 1 Taking Stock

You're new to the job, and the job's new to your company. There are no policies and procedures, no systems information, no real guidelines of any kind for you to follow. The expectations, however, are that you'll change all this. Daunted? Don't be. It's an impressive task, but what a refreshing challenge. How often in life will you again be given the opportunity to create your own universe? If you're tempted to feel sorry for yourself, adrift in this sea of chaos, pity instead the folks who must fill shoes and walk paths worn by generations before them. You have the enviable job of a pioneer: part explorer, part settler, in a whole new and widening world. Before heading out, however, like any prepared pioneer, you'll want to take a bearing on your current location, and take stock of all your inventory. Knowing where you are and what your objectives and priorities are, will better equip you to proceed.

Chapter 1 opens with a description of your mission. It is meant to serve as a starting point with issues worth considering, rather than as a dictum to be swallowed whole. It's your job, your universe. You chart the course in the end, so you need to clearly envision what that end result will look like. The chapter also covers your relationship with the other departments in your organization. To take the explorer analogy just a bit further, consider the different departments in your organization to be parts of a solar system. Some are planets revolving around the sun, some are satellites revolving around larger planets, and some are simply guiding stars to assist you in your own navigation. You need to understand the unique relationships and patterns of movement that exist in your company to function proficiently. In particular, the relationship that exists between you and the mainframe computer department will be a determining factor in your ability to bring about the necessary changes.

Chapter 2 gives you some hints on the types of tools you'll need to get organized. Like the sextant and the captain's log, you'll have your own tools to keep you on track and to serve as guides should you flounder.

One of your first steps will be to conduct an inventory of the existing hardware and software, and to map out where people and systems are. Wiring diagrams and logical groupings will link the individual units of hardware and software to create a map of invaluable worth. Collecting information about the skills and training you have on tap in the people around you is another topic covered in this chapter. The process of gathering this information will further serve to orient you by helping you understand the people you'll be working with.

Chapter 3 describes the importance of establishing various committees and focus groups to help you achieve your various objectives in a shorter time frame. The chapter examines the purpose and nature of these groups, and describes some of the specific groups that you'll want to consider early on.

Part 2   Taking Charge

Part 2 helps you face the tiger calmly. There are three tasks that should be undertaken immediately: you'll need to take inventory of what's around you, you'll need to identify the critical components of your systems, and you'll need to establish the appropriate protection for all systems, particularly the critical ones.

Chapter 4 will help you to gather the information you'll need, including information on hardware, software (commercial and custom), wiring, and people. Chapter 5 will show you how to perform a criticality analysis, and how to identify systems that require maximum uptime and thereby maximum protection from interruption. Security and integrity issues are also addressed, along with the backup implications of your research. Chapter 6 will discuss how to plan for disasters in order to protect your critical systems. The audit process is stressed to ensure that your plan works.

Part 3 The Protective Audits

Once you have completed the immediate steps to ensure that the minimum levels of protection are in place, it's time to turn to other protective audits. Part 3 covers this aspect of your job. You'll learn how to perform and log audits to test backup procedures, virus protection schema, legal liability, and the security of confidential information. You'll also learn what should be performed on a regular basis to prevent hardware failures due to environmental factors, and how to audit source code written by in-house personnel.

Chapter 7 discusses the different types of backup tests that will ensure your data is recoverable. Chapter 8 covers viruses: what to do when you've been hit, how to prevent them, and how to recover from one. Chapter 9 covers the sensitive area of legal liability: what the various policies are, and how to enforce them. If your systems house confidential information, you'll need to perform access audits to ensure that the data is protected from unauthorized access. This subject is covered in Chap. 10.

Chapter 11 covers the various preventive maintenance tasks that should be performed regularly on each machine to avoid hardware failures. Chapter 12 shows you how to hunt down custom applications, and how to manage them for supportability.

Part 4 Support Issues

Most people may recognize your job primarily as a support role, and indeed this is a critical component of your job. Part 4 covers the support aspects of your job, including phone support, training, and communication issues.

Chapter 13 discusses the help desk: how to manage it, and how to get the most out of it. Chapter 14 covers training issues from discovering your company's philosophy to overcoming learning barriers; it also covers training formats, and how to train the trainers. Special skills development is covered in Chap. 15, dealing with special training situations and opportunities. The last chapter in Part 4 discusses your vehicle for communication to the rest of the organization.

Part 5 Performance Issues

Part 5 takes your support one step further to make sure that the various components that make up a user's system is tweaked for maximum productivity gains. Chapter 17 deals with hard-disk maintenance, and shows you how to perform regular audits aimed at maximizing the performance of this potential bottleneck. Chapter 18 deals with the three basic functions carried out by most systems: document management, spreadsheet analysis, and database files. Chapter 19 shows you how to take a look at each department with an eye toward improving efficiency and productivity. The last chapter in this section deals with communication that happens among the various departments and between the organization and the outside world. That chapter will show you how to set up the appropriate communication channels for various types of communication.

Part 6   Strategic Issues

The final section of this book (Part 6) deals with strategic issues. Planning for the future is a part of your job, and the chapters covered here will help you move your organization into the future more smoothly. Chapter 21 shows you how to explore new technology as it becomes available, without wasting time or resources unnecessarily. Chapter 22 deals with the issues of standard setting. Establishing standards will make your job easier, but will leave others unhappy; how to strike a balance between the needs of the corporation and the needs of the individual is discussed, as are the various options at your disposal. As the future unfolds there will be issues as yet unnamed that need to be addressed. Focus studies, the object of Chap. 23, show you how to tackle any issue clearly and quickly. And finally, how to put together your own strategic plan that translates corporate goals into action plans for you and your staff.

Katherine H. Emery

How to Be a Successful Systems Manager in a PC Environment

Introduction

Hiring a Systems Manager— A Note to the Boss

How About Mary, Our Resident Guru?

We'll assume that the reader at this point is a chief financial officer or other higher-level manager who has recently come to the conclusion that someone needs to be in charge of the growing number of microcomputers. The manager's immediate temptation is to assign the job to Mary, whom everyone calls anyway whenever there's a problem. The full-time financial manager becomes, in addition, a part-time computer manager.

It seems like an ideal solution and it may appear to work for a while, but it is not a satisfactory arrangement for two very important reasons: Mary has neither the skills nor the time to do a first-rate job.

First, the financial manager (or chief engineer or office manager) usually lacks the background and specific technical expertise. He or she may have been chosen because his or her computer skills ran the deepest in the organization, but a hacker does not a qualified systems manager make. Would you hire an English major to be your accountant, or ask your accountant to fill in as your lawyer?

Second, computer management functions for these people will always fall to the bottom of their priority list. Critical computer operations such as performing backup audits fall into the C pile—"when I get an extra minute." We all know the extra minute never arrives. At best, the computer management functions are neglected. At worst, the primary responsibilities for which Mary was originally hired also get neglected.

The end result of this type of arrangement is a part-time firefighter, loudly ticking time bombs, and vastly underutilized machines and people. What you need is a professional who has background and expertise in computers and who is dedicated to this function. It may not be a full-time person, and it may not even need to be an employee, but whoever has the role should have systems management as his or her only role.

Help Wanted

What are the qualifications of a good microcomputer manager? A good manager is someone precariously balanced between two worlds. A good systems manager is a people person with a solid technical background. You do not want to fill this position with the stereotypical "techie" who sits behind closed doors ingesting Twinkies and spewing forth code. The job requires lots of people interaction and interest.

At the beginning of your search, determine the minimum technical requirements and add to them strong interpersonal and communications skills. Place an advertisement in the classified section or go through an agency to solicit valid candidates. Ask for résumés to be sent or an application to be completed. Using an application simplifies your next task, which is to weed out candidates who don't fulfill the technical requirements.

The Ad

A typical advertisement might look like this:

> **Computer Systems Manager Sought:**
> Fortune 500 company with over 500 computers seeks person with BS in Computer Science and 3 years' experience in Novell Netware. Experience in manufacturing and PARADOX desired. Strong interpersonal and communications skills required. Please send résumé to . . .

Your list of minimum requirements will help you scan the incoming résumés for applicants you wish to review further. The checklist might look something like this:

- Four-year degree in math or computer science
- Minimum 3.3 GPA
- Minimum work experience—3 years
- Application development experience—2 years
- Strong communications skills
- Strong interpersonal skills

Any résumé failing to meet the minimum technical requirements is eliminated from further review, and initial interviews are scheduled for the remaining candidates. During each interview, the manager will try to get a feel for the interpersonal and communications skills of the applicant, and to get a fuller description of the applicant's previous work experience and reasons for leaving. If during this interview it becomes apparent that the interpersonal skills aren't there, the manager can keep the meeting short and immediately remove the candidate from the list of possible runners.

The Application

Below and on the following pages is an application form that has been expanded into an interview checklist. The first parts may be filled out ahead of the interview, but many of the questions are best asked during

---

Microcomputer Manager Interview Questions

Name:

Address:

Daytime phone:

Evening phone:

List the last 5 companies you worked for and your title and responsibilities there.

1.

2.

3.

4.

5.

Introduction

What degrees or other certification do you hold?				
School	Years	Degree	Major	GPA

What industry experience do you have that would be helpful to you in this job?

What programming languages are you proficient in, and how many years of experience have you accumulated in each?

Language	Years	Experience

What database products are you familiar with, and how many years of experience have you accumulated in each?

Language	Years	Experience

What computer magazines do you read on a regular basis?

Describe the size and complexity of the networks you've worked with in previous jobs.

Why are you considering leaving your current position?

What operating systems are you familiar with?

Operating System	Level of familiarity: 1. Played with it; 2. Strong user; 3. Formal training; 4. Expert level	Years of Experience

Describe your hardware troubleshooting background.

What applications (database, spreadsheets, word processors, etc.) are you familiar with?

Application	Level of familiarity: 1. Played with it; 2. Strong user; 3. Formal training; 4. Expert level	Years of Experience

Would you describe yourself as more . . .

Analytical	or	Creative
Outgoing	or	Introspective
Planner	or	Doer

Would you rather . . .

Teach	or	Program
Design	or	Code
Test code	or	Document code
Provide phone support	or	Debug code

the interview in order to promote conversation on the subject rather than obtain short answers given in isolation.

The Interview

During your interview, pay particular attention to the applicant's communications skills. Listen to the way the applicant talks and listens. Does he or she interrupt you, or consistently misinterpret you, or does the applicant hear your questions and answer you thoughtfully and clearly? Don't be intimidated or impressed by jargon you don't understand. If you can't understand an applicant, it's a bad sign. Ask for clarification, and if the applicant still doesn't make sense, take heed. Remember that no matter how inspired a techno-wonderwiz may be, if people can't understand, or can't stomach listening to the person, progress halts.

Many of the questions you'll ask have no right answer or several ones. Their usefulness lies in their ability to open up the dialogue, in order for you to better gauge the applicant's ability to fit into your organization.

When looking over the specific job experience of any candidate, pay attention to the scope of the tasks and their similarity to your situation and needs. You'll want someone with broad responsibility for a systems configuration similar to yours. A good career path might be from technical assistant to programmer to systems analyst to network administrator to manager. You're looking not only for technical skills but for management experience with demonstrated ability to work well with others.

Real-world expertise will round out an academic background, but it's dangerous to let it substitute for formal schooling. When a nontechnical person is doing the hiring, it can be especially difficult to tell if there are some major gaps in a self-taught person's knowledge base. Although there are bound to be exceptions, your comfort level with a degreed person can be higher in this regard.

Beyond the university degrees, you may find that specific technical certifications apply. Many companies with Novell networks will want a Certified Novell Engineer (CNE), someone who has taken certain courses and passed the tests. Certification will indicate not only a base level of competence but also an ability and willingness to apply oneself to a time-consuming commitment. By asking what industry experience applicants have, you will see how closely related their previous experience may be.

When exploring the programming experience of candidates, have them describe to you the largest application that they have been involved with. Not only will you get a feel for how strong their background is in this area, you'll also see how well they can describe a technical situation in a nontechnical way. The best candidate will be attempting to gauge your level of technical expertise and will match his or her description accordingly. Again, if candidates confuse you, it is more a reflection on their ability to communicate than it is on your intelligence or ability to understand.

Database experience is always important simply because, whether automated or manual, record keeping is core to any organization. Any record-keeping system is in fact a database system, and rare is the organization that doesn't have numerous record-keeping systems. In particular, it will be helpful to have someone who is familiar with the specific products that you have. Realize, however, that someone with a great deal of experience in one database product can transfer that knowledge over much more readily than someone with little or no experience in any database product. Learning your third database is far easier than your second, which is easier by half than your first. (This holds true for any new product in a category of products.)

By finding out what types of magazines the applicant reads, you'll learn a little bit more about the kind of person he or she is. You'll want someone who is up to date on new products and technologies that come on the market. This type of person is usually an avid reader of *PC Magazine, Computer Shopper,* or one of the other technically based periodicals.

If you have a large Novell network in place, you shouldn't talk to anyone without the Novell experience. While applicants may claim that if you've seen one operating system, you've seen them all, you'll run into trouble if you're playing guinea pig while they learn just what the differences are. Some operating systems are similar, and there are many concepts shared by all, but the subtle differences can be significant. If you find the perfect candidate in every respect but this one, remedy the problem with formal training rather than on-the-job experience.

Also keep in mind that managing a five-node network is very different from managing a system with hundreds or thousands of users. The more experience an applicant has with a configuration similar in size and complexity to your own, the more immediately productive he or she will be.

Why is the applicant looking for a job? The answers you'll get may shed some light on problems the applicant has working with people—"My boss is a jerk, always requesting unnecessary reports and asking stupid questions." Some of the answers will surprise you.

Look for a troubleshooting background. It's a large part of the job, and there are few if any university-level courses that offer help in this area. Find out how much experience people have had in this area to help rate the relative strengths among the candidates.

The number and types of applications that your candidate is familiar with will give you an idea of how quickly he or she will come up to speed and be helpful to users. Since 80 percent of typical user questions relate to the first 20 percent of an application's functionality, it won't take long for a strong technical person to come up to speed and have the expertise to field the majority of the questions that users will have. And as already mentioned with respect to database languages, there is a decreasingly steep learning curve presented with each new product in a category of related products. Still, the more directly applicable the experience, the better. Also, the more products a candidate is familiar with overall, the better.

You can add to the either/or questions listed on the application, since some will be more appropriate to your situation than others. These lists are designed to help you identify preferences or personality types that wouldn't otherwise become obvious. For instance, some candidates will be very open in their disdain for documentation, and if they indicate that they would rather die than document, you may take it as a strong indication that they will not be suited to systems management. Often candidates will try to second-guess what you're looking for, so even though they may well have a strong aversion to documentation, they won't say as much if they think it will negatively affect their chances. To reduce the likelihood of this happening, try not to lead the witness. Instead, keep your preferences to yourself. Even when the "right" answer is obvious, these questions can be useful as conversation openers, and as the candidate expands on an answer, you may get some further insight. Shape your questions and your posture to encourage applicants to talk. The more they talk, the more you learn.

Candidates who pass this level of screening should exhibit strong interpersonal and communications skills and appear to you to be technically competent. Further interviews with additional members of your staff, tests to objectively measure the technical skills, and reference calls should all follow to help you accurately rate the candidates and select the best person for the job.

Here, then, in summary are the steps in the hiring process:

1. Determine minimum requirements.
2. Place ad requesting résumés.
3. Eliminate candidates on the basis of minimum technical requirements.

4. Set up initial interviews.
5. Eliminate candidates on the basis of interpersonal skills and further investigation of technical qualifications.
6. Hold a second interview with promising candidates and obtain more detailed analysis of technical skills.
7. Check references.
8. Rate candidates and make the final selection.

Orientation

Once you've brought a new systems manager on board, make sure that he or she is properly oriented to your organization and is getting a feel for all the ways in which computers are being used today. Consider having the new systems manager spend time in each department during an orientation period, to become familiar with what is done there and with how computers are being used. Without a global view of the organization and a real understanding of the business, a systems manager cannot be expected to be long-sighted in strategic planning, or even effective in providing short-term solutions to existing problems.

In the end, you're looking for someone whom you feel comfortable working with, who has a strong technical background, and who shows signs of being an organized, motivated, and motivating person.

Part

1

Taking Stock

Chapter 1

Your Mission

Your mission, should you decide to accept it, will be to harness the tremendous power of your organization's microcomputers. It is a noble and many-faceted mission. If you are successful, many people will be both grateful and indebted to you for making their lives easier, more productive, and more profitable. This book is intended to help you in your work, by enumerating the tasks at hand and providing the tools to achieve your goals. It is truly not just a job. You are the microcomputer systems manager.

Past Is Prologue—The History of Information Systems

Your role will be perceived very differently from company to company, depending in part on when and how computers have been integrated into the organization in the past. Below are some of the relationships that exist, shown in the order in which they have generally been introduced into corporate organizational charts.

The most traditional relationship (Fig. 1.1) shows information systems (IS) reporting to the chief financial officer (CFO). When the sole purpose of the computer was for accounting, this arrangement made perfect sense. There was no differentiation between the mainframe and the micro department because there were no micros.

As the PC became more prevalent, a separate PC division was often split off (Fig. 1.2). The micro department was often created to off-load the pesky problems that end users and PCs caused, in order to leave the mainframe people free to attend to serious computing problems.

As computers grew beyond the scope of financial systems, some com-

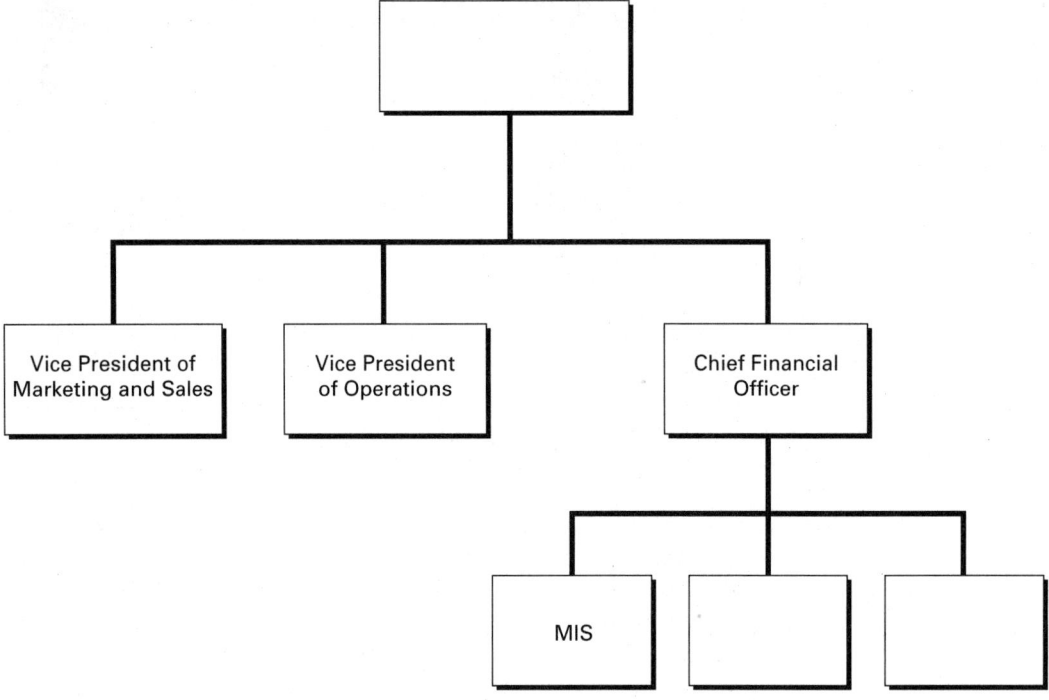

Figure 1.1 Management information systems reporting to CFO.

panies more appropriately put the IS function on a par with the financial department, rather than subservient to it (Fig. 1.3).

Today, more and more you will see a scenario in which the central IS department is still apparent but is combined with the concept of departmental IS functions (Fig. 1.4). The corporate IS division then takes more of a strategic and planning role, defining global parameters, and leaving the departmental units free to act independently for the good of the departments they serve.

Get a copy of your company's organizational chart, and find out which model is used. If there is no such chart available, have your supervisor help you sketch one. It will tell you a lot about the way the company perceives your mission. This isn't to say that you can't or won't change those perceptions (and your position on the chart) over time if they don't facilitate your taking on the challenge of your full potential. The chart should give you some advance notice as to whether you'll encounter any immediate resistance from parties who may feel that you're overstepping your bounds.

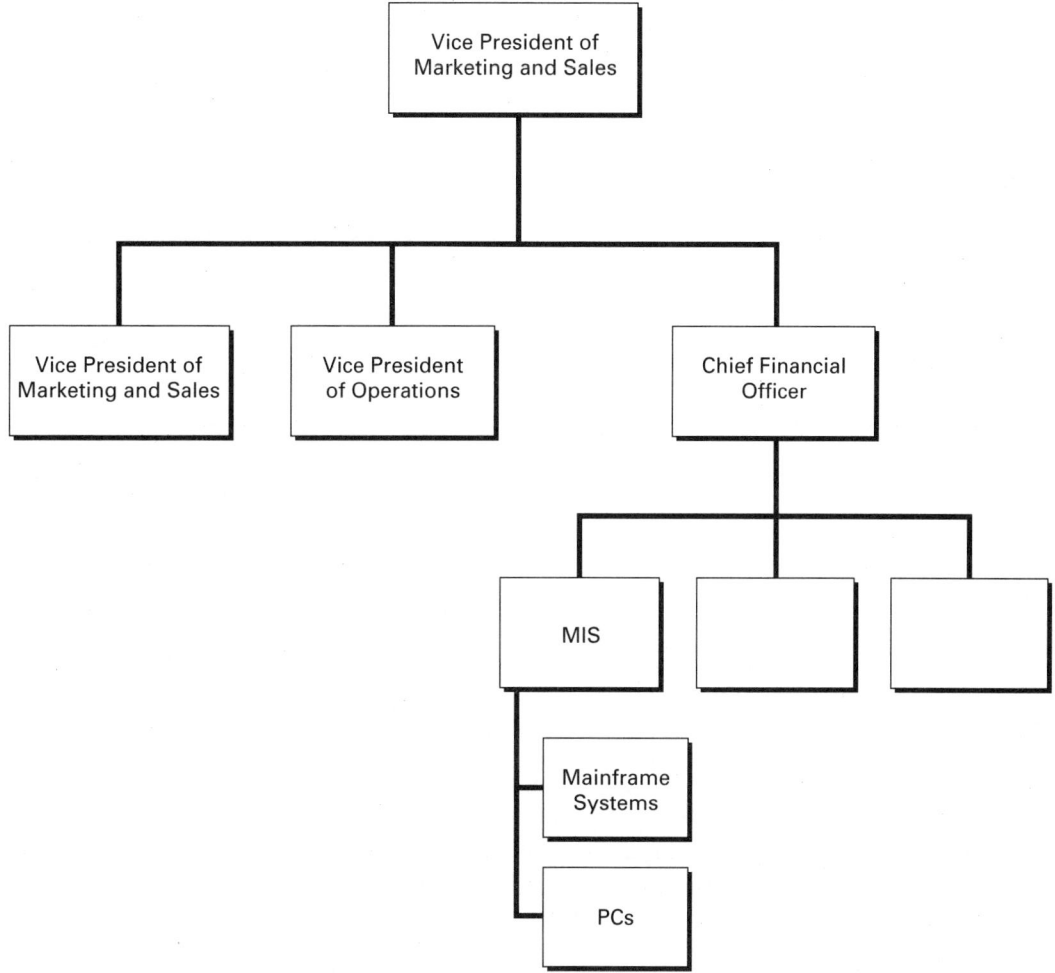

Figure 1.2 In time, separate PC divisions were created.

You and IS or You Is IS

If you report to the IS director of a predominantly mainframe shop, your relationship may most closely resemble that of the ugly stepchild. It's an all too common relationship that comes about when an MIS (management information systems) department is staffed by mainframers who are unfamiliar (and therefore uncomfortable) with PCs. These professionals, a rapidly dying breed, are still of the mind-set that microcomputers are pesky lightweights. Preferring not to sully their

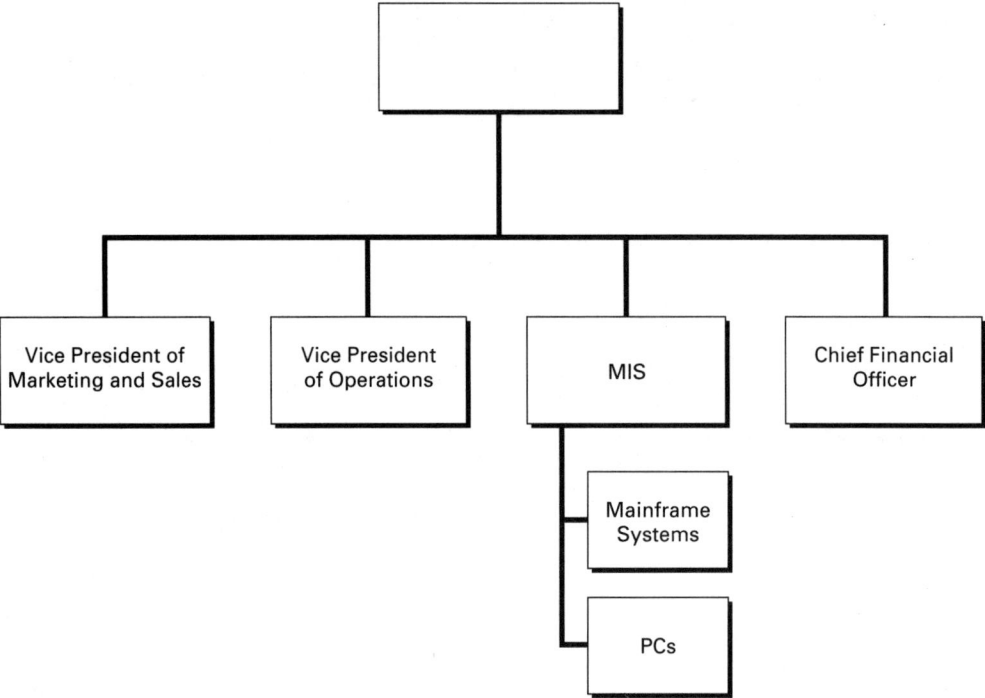

Figure 1.3 As computers grew, companies put the IS function on a par with their financial department.

hands with PC work, they have assigned you to the job of keeping PC questions and problems from landing on their doorstep. Your comments and suggestions on "managing" these systems will be met with hostility regardless of their merit, and the less the MIS folks see of you, the more they'll like you. Your strategic-planning efforts will be thwarted, and even your performance-tuning plans will be shunted aside to the degree that they threaten the territory covered by MIS.

If you are not under the MIS thumb, but have been brought in to stand alongside the existing IS department, then your relationship may more closely resemble that of the ugly stepsister. This may be every bit and perhaps even more hostile than the stepchild relationship because you are on equal footing as far as some higher-up is concerned, and you will get little if any cooperation from IS when it comes to working out solutions to organizational problems. You'll be seen as the little sister and hopefully tolerated as such. You will have to work together, in collusion, or at odds. Obviously, the friendlier you are, the better it will be for all concerned. First impressions are important. If you see from the organizational chart that you're not the only computer support unit within the company, take heed. Try to ingratiate yourself, showing that

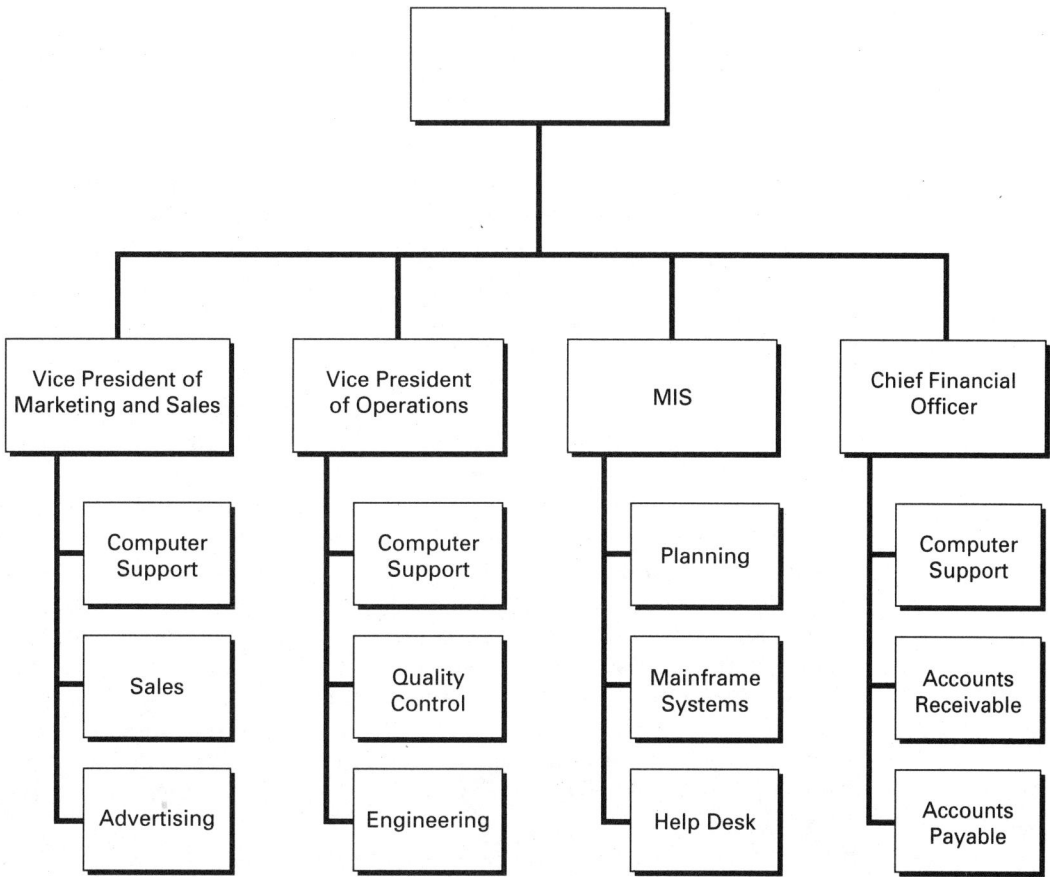

Figure 1.4 The central IS department is now combined with departmental IS functions.

you are interested in a cooperative rather than competitive relationship. If you come charging in, full of great ideas, you'll be perceived as a threat, regardless of your intentions. Instead, find out all you can about the efforts that this group is involved with and throw your weight into helping others where you can. By helping others look good, you're more likely to get cooperation when you need it.

If the introduction of computers in your organization has been limited to PCs, you may be lucky enough to be an only child—with no other computer-related department to deal with. This is a wonderful place to be from a systems manager's view. You have the freedom to be as helpful as you can without worrying about stepping on anyone's toes. In fact, while the downsizing of big, old companies has created offshoots of microcomputer departments from the original IS group, the more common phenomenon in new and growing companies will be to see mature microcomputer departments spawning mainframe or minicomputer subcomponents. With the shoe on the other foot, let's hope we as microcomputer managers won't repeat the sins of our forebears.

In the beginning, your role may be circumscribed by your relationship with and placement among the other departments in your organization. Regardless, you should have in mind the full scope of your mission and push to mold it over time until it encompasses the full range of responsibilities that fall under the charge of systems management.

What Your Job Is and What It Is Not

Your mission, again, is to harness the tremendous power of your organization's microcomputers. Do not confuse the verb *to harness* with the verb *to restrain*. If your job were merely computer cop—making sure no one bought any unauthorized hardware or software, or played any unauthorized games during office hours—a whip would be more appropriate than this book. You will have to deal with the issue of control. Semantics have a way of predisposing our way of thinking, and there are many employees who consider the corporate microcomputer to be their own personal computer. This mode of thinking isn't valid in an organizational environment, and at times, for the good of the many, the rights of the individual may have to be superseded. Under this burden of responsibility you will tread lightly, but you must be strong. Armed with good reason, you will be able to justify your role in this function to others.

But this position is no place for anyone with a bent for control. While there are aspects of control to be considered, your primary role is that of an enabler. You're going to help your fellow employees and the organization you work for step boldly ahead using the technology available to them. It is a positive, creative, and challenging role.

Your mission is to harness these machines in order to make use of their power, as one would harness the wind to make the windmills fly. The corporate computer can do many many things, and it is not likely that all the potential uses for it are now being explored in your organization. It is your job to help discover these unknown pockets of power, recognize their potential, liberate them, and use them to realize the goals of the company.

Four Prime Objectives

Your first objective must be protection. In an unprotected environment nothing can be accomplished. As in Maslow's hierarchy of needs, you must provide a base of security for your users or no one will feel comfortable venturing forward with technology. You are responsible for creating a safe environment through:

- Protection of physical assets from theft, damage, and unnecessary wear and tear
- Protection of data against unauthorized access, destruction, or corruption
- Protection of people against inaccessible, invalid, or unusable information

A second critical objective will be to constantly strive for improved performance. The ever-changing environment in which you are operating will require you to continuously monitor and refocus your efforts. It is more of a process than an obtainable goal, but the focus is always on peak performance.

Supporting your clients is a third objective. You need to be responsive to your fellow staff. They are in a sense your clients, and you are in a consulting business that depends on your clients' satisfaction. Many an information center has disappeared, and plenty put themselves out of a job, when they began to take the "don't bother me" attitude. If your clients don't feel comfortable going to you for advice and help, you will find yourself without clients, and it won't take too long before the company decides it can do without you. You are responsible for creating an environment in which corporate employees are getting the information and the automation they need to maximize their potential. Your aim is to make them happier, more productive, more enthusiastic, and more enlightened about the resource they have at their disposal through computer access.

Finally, you must use automation to help achieve the strategic goals of your organization. You will need to stay up to date on the technical advancements being made every day in hardware and software, and you must pay particular attention to new technologies that might have an impact (positive or negative) on your organization as well as on your own computer systems management goals.

The moment you were hired, someone breathed a sigh of relief as the fuzzy black cloud of worry disappeared, or rather shuffled on over to rain on your shoulders. Welcome to the job!

Don't Grab the Tiger Yet

No doubt, your first day will be spent listening to many problems and concerns, the backlog of which has accumulated over perhaps years, and now is finally unleashed upon you. Your impulse will be to rush like the knight in shining armor (as undoubtedly you will be perceived) to solve all the problems, and win the hearts of everyone you meet. Do it. Go ahead and solve anything you can with a wave of your wand or 5 minutes of your time, but for anything requiring longer periods of time make a list, prioritize the items, and schedule part of your day for solving each and every one. But remember that part of your day (at least half) needs to be spent on proactive planning. If you don't put it in your schedule, you'll be reacting forever. Many systems managers have retired early, exhausted, burned out, because rather than planning their attack they grabbed the tiger by the tail.

Your job will always be somewhat ad hoc. Still, no matter how forcefully the day-to-day problems pull you around willy-nilly, you have to exert an equal force in the opposite direction of planning and control. You must start putting systems into place from day one, with the goal in mind of heading off potential problems, and working toward improved systems performance. The first step in this process is to assess where you are right now. This is covered in Part 2, Taking Charge. You need to know where you are now before you can plan properly for your future.

The Mission Statement

Here at the threshold is a good time to examine your purpose and goals. You may not be aware of specific problems that await you and exactly what priorities will make the most sense. But you ought to be able to articulate, in the form of a mission statement, what you intend to accomplish from a global perspective. The statement doesn't have to be overly long and formal, but it should clearly explain your role as you see it. The exercise will force you to define and describe your mission. Without going through this exercise, without having a clear picture in your mind as to what you are planning to accomplish, you have very little chance of getting there.

The mission statement, while open to evolutionary changes over time, should remain fairly constant in its ability to describe your overriding purpose. You can follow through on this statement with specific objectives and goals that in turn translate to action plans for the next several months or years. These plans will address specific projects designed to fulfill your mission. They can and will change radically from one year to the next, as the specific crises and opportunities appear on the horizon. The development of action plans will have to wait until you have a better understanding of your surroundings. By contrast, the

> **Sample Mission Statement for Microcomputer Systems Management**
>
> We are responsible for the microcomputer systems throughout the corporate headquarters and our mission has four primary objectives:
>
> 1. *Protection.* We will protect the corporation from loss of data and unnecessary downtime caused by hardware and software failures. We will ensure that sensitive corporate data are secure from unauthorized access.
>
> 2. *Support.* We will provide users of corporate computers with the assistance they need to perform their jobs in a timely, helpful manner. We will encourage the use of new technology and tools to enhance productivity and other corporate goals, and we will help users develop their own technical knowledge.
>
> 3. *Performance tuning.* We will strive to improve our performance and efficiency of computer operations as well as manual information systems through further automation and improved procedures and technology.
>
> 4. *Strategic planning.* We will work to uncover new ways to use existing hardware, software, data, and personnel to achieve the strategic goals of our firm, which are:
>   —Increase sales.
>   —Improve customer satisfaction.
>   —Improve the perceived quality of our products.
>
> Signed: _____ Date: _____
>
> Approved: _____ Date: _____

creation of the mission statement is best done before heading into the trees, while the forest is still visible to you.

Upon completing your mission statement, review it with your manager. The statement will show your supervisor that you are well organized and will give him or her an opportunity to buy into your goals. If you take the initiative at this point, your statement is likely to be approved. Later, when you need to be able to defend a given action plan, you can point to the specific goal in your mission statement that supports the action plan.

The Action Plans

Specific goals flow from your mission statement, and developing these goals is a part of your own annual strategic planning process. The mission statement provides overall guidelines only. Your specific goals will result in detailed action plans to be carried out over the coming year.

Ideally, your mission statement and action plans will be used to measure your performance over the course of the year. Your mission statement will tell people why you are doing what you do. Your action plans will tell people specifically what you plan to do—and your accomplishments will speak for themselves.

At the end of your first year, you will be better able to put together a complete strategic plan, because you will have a much better feel for the problems and opportunities you face and their respective priorities. Upon your arrival you need to establish your initial goals and plans of action. Because of your lack of information, your initial plans will be fewer in number and less detailed than the ones to follow.

Your initial set of action plans should include three basic goals:

- To develop an inventory of the various systems within your domain
- To perform a criticality analysis in order to ascertain where the high-risk areas are
- To begin development of a disaster plan which provides adequate coverage for those high-risk areas

These are the first goals for any new systems manager. They should take the highest priority, since they provide the most basic level of protection for your users. With these three goals, you can flesh out specific action plans.

Each action plan should relate to a specific goal or goals in your mission statement. If you have a hard time making a match, then either your mission statement is inadequate or (more likely) the action plan is suspect. Further, each action plan should have specific, quantifiable deliverables, or outcomes, by which you can measure the success of the plan itself. An outcome may be a document, the installation of a new piece of software, or the fact that training has occurred for certain segments of the staff. In any case, achievement of the outcome should point to the successful completion of the action plan itself.

A schedule, budget, and list of responsibilities should also be included. If more than one person is involved in achieving a goal, an action plan manager should be assigned with overall responsibility for the eventual outcome. Without a manager, the plan can get stalled among players, with no one person feeling responsible for picking up the ball.

The following two action plans complement the mission statement shown above by responding to one or more of its primary objectives.

So welcome, good luck, and remember your challenge: Protect your systems. Support them. Make them sing!

> **Sample 1994 Action Plans for Microcomputer Systems Management**
>
> **Description:** Develop a disaster plan
>
> **How it advances our mission:** The plan will ensure that any extreme situation that renders our existing facility useless will not interrupt the critical functions of our microcomputer data-processing capacity.
>
> **Outcomes:** Disaster plan
> Disaster drill plan and schedule
> Budget for implementation
>
> **Time frame:** To be completed by the end of 1994
>
> **Cost:** Unknown at this point
>
> **Project manager:** Francis Bagon
>
> **Responsibilities:** Frank Bagon will bring together and head up the disaster planning committee, and a more complete list of responsibilities will follow early meetings of this committee.
>
> ---
>
> **Description:** Develop a help desk plan
>
> **How it advances our mission:** The help desk will support end users more efficiently and effectively by accumulating data on common problems and trends so that proactive measures can be taken.
>
> **Outcomes:** Help desk organizational plan
> Schedule and budget for implementation
>
> **Time frame:** To be completed by the end of 1994
>
> **Cost:** Unknown at this point
>
> **Project manager:** Geraldine Hanvey
>
> **Responsibilities:** Gerrie Hanvey will put together a plan for the organization and staffing of a help desk, along with a budget and schedule for implementation.

To Do

- Get an organization chart and see where I am.
- Develop a mission statement and initial action plans.
- Review statement and plans with supervisor and revise.

Chapter 2

Getting Organized

Ready, Set . . .

It's the Olympic women's 10K race: "Ready? Set? Go!" And they're off. Down the track, around the bend. Sleek bodies in crisp shorts, a blur past the grandstands, flying past the admiring crowd and old speed records. Around they go until the final lap, with the finish line in sight. One runner is slightly ahead of the rest—teeth bared, half grimace, half grin—knowing that the ribbon, the race, is hers. The cameras flash, capturing the winner's arms raised in victory, the sweat, the muscles still straining, the eyes gleaming in the knowledge that all the hard hours have finally paid off, that the rest of the world is seeing what she has played in her mind over and over again.

Now it's your turn. Your race is not unlike an athlete's and requires no less visualization and preparation to make it happen. If you start with the "go" phase, you'll never get back to the ready and the set, or the vision that prepares a real winner. You'll merely go—for 8 hours a day, 52 paychecks a year. Then, some frightful day, you'll look back on it all and wonder where your life dropped away.

If, on the other hand, you start with a picture of what you want to accomplish, you'll be racing toward something. You'll know when you've reached your goal. It begins with visualization. In the preceding chapter you defined your mission, creating a mental picture of what your objectives are. Now you need to equip yourself with the tools and information you need to accomplish your mission, and to organize these pieces into an effective whole.

Tao of Systems Management

The key to an athlete's success is visualization, followed by the development of specific athletic skills, strength, and stamina. What you as a systems manager accomplish will be determined no less by your vision, followed by your development of specific management skills, diplomacy, and follow-through.

This chapter covers some of the basic organizational tools that will help get you off on the right foot. In later chapters we will more fully examine your repertoire of systems management skills, reviewing as well issues of diplomacy and tact. (Your basic interpersonal skills are assumed, since these are prerequisite to the position you're in.) Follow-through is one of the hardest skills to teach but among the most desirable to possess, because without it the best ideas go nowhere. Certainly key to the successful completion of any task is developing a plan with specific goals, establishing deadlines, and reviewing your success regularly. These concepts and techniques are also covered here and in later chapters.

There's no magic involved, no systems management software that will make it all happen with a few keystrokes. It's equal parts art, science, and organization.

The Systems Profile

We'll begin with the systems profile binder, which attempts to maintain a profile or sketch of the systems you are responsible for. Whether you choose to collect and organize information in binders and folders on your desk or electronically is up to you. Whatever does the job most quickly carries the advantage of getting you up and into action sooner, but you also have to be aware of the role model you represent. The manual icons will be discussed here for simplicity's sake. However, realize that automated systems will give you much greater flexibility and functionality.

You've already examined or created an organizational chart. This is the first thing you'll put in your systems profile binder, which will store all the information you collect about hardware, software, people, and connections. The profile is a map of your terrain. Gathering the information you need to complete it will familiarize you with the lay of the land.

Put your organizational chart behind a tab marked Personnel, along with a listing of the personnel in each departmental (include titles and phone numbers). A simple alphabetic directory of the whole organization will also be helpful. Next, behind a tab marked Layouts, include anything that gives a physical picture of your territory. A floor layout will be helpful, not only to find out who is where, but also to serve as a backdrop for your wiring plan and your equipment. Floor plans may already be available to you; ask the building superintendent. If they're not, you will need to develop them as you take inventory.

Hardware and Software tabs will follow. This information will also be gathered as you complete your inventory. Even if lists are available here, you should assume that they are not up to date.

The Master Planner

Your Master Planner binder will have tabs marked Goals, Open Items, Plans, Calendar, and Logs. Put your mission statement and goals in the front section so you'll be forced to see them daily.

The Open section of your master planner will keep any to-do items that haven't yet been planned. (See the end-of-chapter to-do lists throughout this book). When a good idea comes up, write it down here quickly so it doesn't get lost before you have time to think it through, develop a plan, and fit it into your schedule. Your Open Items list will help remind you. Your mission statement goes in the Goals section of this binder to serve as a constant reminder of your goals and objectives.

Once you have developed ideas into projects by developing action plans, you'll put them in priority order in the Plans section of your master planner and cross them off your Open Items list. In the beginning, you may have only your first three action plans—take inventory, perform a criticality analysis, and develop a disaster plan—but over time this section will grow. Each action plan should include specific deliverables, dates, responsibilities, and milestones when appropriate.

In your Calendar section, develop a master schedule for each person on your team, broken down by month. This section may be limited to yourself in the beginning; but as your committees become active and as your staff grows, so will the number of calendars. As projects are developed, you'll use the master calendar to check for scheduling conflicts and to post milestones and other due dates accordingly. You'll do plenty of rearranging as your master plan develops and contingencies have to be accounted for. Unless you plan, however, chaos will eventually prevail.

Strive to maintain a master calendar that has milestones evenly distributed over the course of the year, with no one month having more milestones than you feel is manageable. Remember that these are your planned activities. There will be no predicting (or stopping) the unplanned fires that you'll have to put out. So you'll need to leave room for the inevitable and build in flexibility overall if you want to avoid

Systems Manager's Log				
Date	Project/Service Request	Hours	Dept.	Activity

ulcers and other stress-related illnesses. Review your progress weekly or monthly. Check off what has been done and make any necessary revisions in the schedule for future months.

In the Logs section of your master planner, keep a history of what you spend your time on. In your systems manager's log, list the times and projects or problems that you handle to see exactly what you're spending time on. The list will help you plan in the future. Track the hours, the department, and the type of work. At the end of the year, you'll be able to generate reports showing how much time you spend responding to emergencies, how much time you spend planning, and so on.

You may also wish to keep a service request log to ensure that no client problem or request falls between the cracks. When you receive a service request, give it a number, log the date opened, assign a priority, and give a brief description of the request. When the service request is resolved, note the date closed. Some organizations use E-mail or a central database on the network to log requests.

The Project Folder

Once you have completed a basic action plan, you'll want to put together a project folder and start filling in the details. Begin by identifying the specific steps or tasks that make up the project so that you can better visualize the whole process. Reaching the goal then becomes simply a matter of following the steps. This process of breaking down a large job into many smaller tasks is the secret to accomplishing any

| Service Request Log ||||||
No.	Opened	Priority	Description		Closed

seemingly impossible job. Whenever you're faced with some insurmountable task that you keep planning to begin, but somehow never do, try dissecting the whole into parts and attacking the parts separately. Mount Everest, as you've probably heard tell, is scaled step by step. The steps that you might identify in developing a disaster plan include:

1. Take immediate action to forestall disaster now.
2. Identify committee members.
3. Prepare goal statement.
4. Identify systems at risk.
5. Identify sources of risk.
6. Identify ways to reduce risk.
7. Identify recovery requirement levels.
8. Identify means to achieve recovery requirements.
9. Develop notification plans and contingencies.
10. Develop testing plans and schedule.
11. Make first draft of plan.
12. Review plan and make corrections.
13. Prepare final draft.
14. Set review date.

Action Plan: Develop a Disaster Plan			
Who	Due	Done	Description/Detail
Self	Jan.		Take immediate action to forestall disaster now.
Self	Jan.		Identify committee members. Choose representatives from each department.
Self	Jan.		Prepare goal statement. Review with committee and make changes as needed.
Self	Jan.		Identify systems at risk by auditing each department.
Self	Feb.		Identify sources of risk. Compile list and review with committee members.
Self	Feb.		Identify ways to reduce risk. Compile recommendations and review with committee members.
Self	Feb.		Identify recovery requirement levels. Establish levels of risk and have committee members make assignments. Review and approve each risk level as a committee.
Self	Mar.		Identify means to achieve recovery requirements. Establish recovery plan and review with committee.
Self	Mar.		Establish notification plans and contingencies and review with committee.
Self	Mar.		Establish adequate testing plans and review them with the committee. Set up schedules for both planned and surprise tests of various kinds.
Self	Apr.		Prepare first draft of plan and present it to the committee for approval.
?	May		Obtain reviews and make corrections. If possible, use outside consultants. Present revisions to the committee.
Self	June		Prepare final draft and present it to the committee.
Self	June		Set review date and kick off testing phase.

Once you have identified specific steps, you can better determine who needs to be involved and how long any one step is going to take. In cases where timing is critical, assign the completion dates first and then assign responsibilities as necessary in order to meet the schedule. If you have limited staff (only yourself?), you'll have to let the schedule fall where it may. Responsibilities and dates can and will be shifted after the original assignments have been made. Still, enough slack time should be built into the original schedule so that changes are kept to a minimum. Too much slippage leads to sloppiness.

The complications involved in dealing with a large number of people and tasks can quickly make a manual system unwieldy. An automated project manager will help you in setting up projects with subtasks and will allow you to manage them along the way, creating reports and calendars and facilitating changes.

There will be tasks that have prerequisite tasks, or you'll find that what first appears to be an isolated project is really better broken into several subprojects. Any task may become a project in and of itself if it has subtasks and a deliverable all its own. For instance, the first task in the development of a disaster plan—to take immediate action to forestall disaster now—could become a project in itself. Substeps would include identifying critical systems, establishing backups, and storing them off-site. The deliverable is the off-site backups. In general, the fewer the subtasks the better. Rolling up too many subtasks under one heading runs the risk of creating another undefeatable monster. Consider breaking up any task when more than one responsible party, deliverable, or due date is involved. The project leader (often you) will keep plans, correspondence, meeting minutes, and any other project notes in the project folder.

The systems profile, master planner, and project folder are your primary organizational tools. You'll also want to set up your users to facilitate your support function.

\multicolumn{4}{c}{**Backup Log**}			
Date	Set	Initials	Comments

Significant Events Log			
Date	Type	Initials	Comments

The Workstation Folder

To help organize your users, make up a folder for each computer. A pocket binder taped to the side of the terminal is most effective. In the pocket, place a boot disk and several logs, as described below.

The backup log (see page 31) tracks backups for which the user is responsible. (The log is not necessary if backups are done centrally.) It should include the date of the backup, the backup set that was used,

Preventive Maintenance Log		
Date	Initials	Comments

the initials or signature of the person doing the backup, and any comments that may be relevant, such as error messages or warnings.

The significant events log shows problems, changes, and other significant events in chronological order. The preventive maintenance log shows when preventive maintenance functions were performed on the computer. You might use the following shorthand to describe the type of maintenance work performed:

$$P = problem$$
$$CS = change\ in\ software$$
$$CH = change\ in\ hardware$$

There should also be a stack of service request forms that will enable your clients to list all the information you'll need when they have a problem or request for you to work on. When a user logs a service request, ask that one copy be kept with the machine and the other forwarded to you. If the problem isn't an emergency, the service request will remain in the Open Items section of your master planner until it is resolved. This form should have the date, CPU number, and requester's name, phone, and department. A description of the problem and the level of urgency should follow.

These are some of the basic tools that will help you get organized and stay in control. In the next chapter we'll look at working with people. The technician in you may prefer to do it all yourself, but the manager in you should realize that the only way to accomplish all that you need to accomplish, in any reasonable period of time, is with other people's help.

It starts with a mission and an action plan and gains momentum as

Service Request		
Date:	Requested by:	
CPU number:	Department/phone:	
Request:		
Priority:	Completion date:	By:
Reason:		
Details:		

you organize teams to help you. If you have done the planning and the visualizing up front, you'll be able to accomplish Olympian feats in the arena of systems management.

To Do

- Create systems profile binder.
- Get departmental listings and phone directory.
- Find out if superintendent has floor plans.
- Create master planner.
- Set up master calendars for everyone.
- Start keeping a log.
- Make up project folders for first three projects.
- Create workstation folders.

Chapter 3

Working Through Committees

Your Nemesis, Your Salvation

Bringing together and managing people through committees is going to be one of your biggest challenges. People are infinitely more surprising and complex than computers, and therefore more difficult to manage, but don't make the mistake of assuming that you can do without them. You'll get less done over a longer time period, and your results will be not be recognized for their full worth. Carefully orchestrated, committees can yield you tremendous payback in synergistic enthusiasm and involvement. If you make all the decisions on your own, things may happen more quickly but they won't be as well thought out or as well accepted.

Some committees will be ongoing, year after year, addressing changing issues and recurring needs. Other committees will spring up out of a particular need, and should disband once the initial goal of the committee has been achieved. If you've never worked through committees before, here are some things you'll want to think about before calling your first meeting.

Committee Etiquette

There is nothing more irritating than being dragged into a meeting that has no point to begin with and wanders endlessly from there. We all hate having our time wasted. Remember this any time people must be brought together. Make sure there is a reason for the committee that you are about to assemble. Write down the mission statement for the committee, briefly and without any unnecessary jargon or puffing. Obviously, if you have no good reason for creating a committee, don't.

Once you've defined the committee's raison d'être, you'll have to determine who should serve. Who understands the issues? People come to the table with very different orientations, skills, and backgrounds, and this is good. It is, in fact, why you are bringing them together. A good balance in these areas is the key to a good committee, as is a willingness and an ability to work with the group. The "one bad apple" phenomenon is nowhere as evident as in the committee setting. Theoretically, the committee's purpose is all that should matter, but in the real world you'll have to consider the political implications as well. For instance, when decisions will be made that affect a particular department, that department should have representation on the committee, regardless of other considerations. Without departmental involvement, it will be difficult carrying out any decisions made. In some cases, you won't be able to pick and choose your players. Whenever you can choose, learn as much as possible about a person before asking for involvement.

Your role as committee chair should be to facilitate discussion, generate consensus, and achieve the objectives set forth. Your first meeting will set the precedent for future meetings. You'll need to explain up front, in a memo, what the purpose of the committee is (very briefly) and what the agenda for the first meeting will be. Include the time, date, location, and duration of the meeting along with the topics to be discussed. Come prepared, so you're not wasting anyone's time. Stick to the agenda. People like to know what to expect, and are grateful when you give them what they expected. Get participation. If you actively involve people, they will take ownership of the issues. If you or any other member takes up too much time at the podium, you'll be facing more feeble excuses and empty chairs with every new meeting. Build consensus. Let the various views be expressed, and try to bring out the commonalities that exist in order to move the group toward decisions. Discussion is vital, but endless debates are debilitating. If consensus cannot be reached after a limited time, take a vote.

Be on the lookout for red herring questions or other tangential discourse that leads the group off track. You'll want to swing back as tactfully as possible. Some effective derailers that don't necessarily injure egos include:

"Good point. Could you write up a summary on that issue for everyone?"

"I think this issue, while important, is better handled off-line. Could I ask anyone interested in more discussion on the subject to bring it up with Dave directly after the meeting?"

"I'm afraid we have to move on now, or we won't be able to stick to the agenda we've set. Let's wrap up with any questions that anyone else has. If need be, we can put Carla's issue on our agenda for next month."

Be especially wary of the research hound—the one who delights in saying "I think we should look into . . . " for no other reason than to watch everyone scramble. This person can have the committee chasing after all kinds of useless facts and wasting endless amounts of time. The easiest way to defend against such behavior is to assign at least the initial preparation to the person who suggests the research. Once research hounds realize that they will be the first to be dumped on, they're likely to calm down.

Whenever possible, limit your meetings to 90 minutes or less. If regular meetings are consistently running over, consider increasing the frequency of the meetings rather than lengthening the time slot. There is often a good reason for a couple of long sessions—for example, year-end planning or crisis handling. In these cases, however, you should call a special session, letting people know that the meeting will be a long one. The more frequently a committee meets, the shorter the meetings should be.

Keep the committee notes on file along with a list of action items. Each action item should have a responsible party and the expected turnaround date. Open each meeting with any old business that needs to be addressed, including action items that require attention.

If you will be calling on people to make reports, forewarn them with a phone call a few days before the meeting. If you surprise people at a meeting when they have not done their homework, you will embarrass and antagonize them to no good purpose. Give them some notice, however, and they will most likely make a last-minute scramble to have their responsibilities covered. If they do, they look good in the meeting and you've accomplished your objective. If they don't, they're embarrassed publicly, as they should be; but they can't blame you for taking them by surprise.

You can run your meetings by parliamentary rules or by the seat of your pants. Whatever you decide, *lead* your meetings. If you've ever been in a meeting that drifts down countless side channels and gets swept up in endless whirlpools of discussion, you know why people hate meetings. Keep the agenda short and to the point, and people will love you for it.

The Security Committee and the Planning Committee are especially important, since they focus on two of your primary objectives and have several subcommittees beneath them. We'll look at each in turn, along with the audits they perform.

The Security Committee

The Security Committee is concerned with data protection. It should be made up of high-level management from each department—simply because the decisions made at this level cannot be delegated.

The first meeting can convene as soon as you've completed the inventory and begun the criticality analysis. You will address the findings of these two projects, and set the agenda for future meetings. You may be able to develop a comprehensive agenda for the year, setting broad goals and identifying projects. Keep in mind, however, that unplanned-for issues will undoubtedly arise throughout the year.

The Security Committee should meet every month initially but can eventually fall back to a bimonthly or quarterly schedule. The committee will probably need to spawn several subcommittees to address disaster planning, legal issues, insurance issues, and routine maintenance.

The disaster planning subcommittee should consist of members of all departments. In this way, the special needs of each department will be taken into consideration, and the committee will have a spokesperson for each department who coordinates the disaster efforts. The initial role of this subcommittee is to establish the disaster plan for the company, and to ensure that the necessary steps are taken to implement the plan. During the development of the organization's first disaster plan, this subcommittee needs to meet frequently. Even when a plan is in place, the group needs to meet monthly in order to update the plan. The subcommittee must also review the results of the various disaster drills, which are usually conducted once per quarter.

The legal issues subcommittee usually meets twice per year, unless specific problems need more immediate resolution. One of the key concerns of the subcommittee is the use of unauthorized software on corporate machines. This group will establish the means for monitoring compliance with the company's policies regarding copyright issues. It will also analyze the results of its legal liability audits, which are usually held twice a year.

The insurance issues subcommittee is responsible for ensuring that adequate insurance coverage exists and that all contingencies have been considered. Preventing undercoverage as well as overcoverage requires continual monitoring, because of changing regulations and the value of covered equipment. This subcommittee usually needs to meet only twice per year and to hold one audit anually.

The routine maintenance subcommittee schedules and analyzes the results of the various routine audits aimed at preventing problems. These include:

- Annual power audits to verify that existing buffers will guard against power surges and sags
- Annual backup audits to determine if backups are being performed and if the backups are indeed restorable
- Six-month viral audits to determine and remove the existence of any viral infections
- Six-month preventive maintenance audits to clean and otherwise maintain hardware components

Depending on the results of these audits, the subcommittee will need to take additional action and schedule meetings more or less frequently. Quarterly meetings are typical.

The Planning Committee

Even though all committees must deal in some fashion with planning, the formal Planning Committee is responsible for developing the guidelines that move the technology forward to help achieve corporate objectives as they evolve. Without this committee's work, investments would continue to be made in dying technology, or in new but irrelevant technology, and the past and future would be linked by giant leaps from one dead end to another. This committee is responsible for drawing together ideas from all over the organization and outside world into a cohesive, comprehensive, manageable plan. It too has several subcommittees.

The new technology review subcommittee should be constantly surveying the outside world for new technology that could help the organization compete and better serve its customer. This subcommittee should meet every 2 months to review findings and make recommendations.

The help desk review subcommittee focuses on prevention. Depending on the issues that arise at the help desk, this subcommittee will make recommendations for training and other proactive measures to better serve end users and to preempt avoidable problems. This subcommittee too should meet every 2 months.

The communications subcommittee usually meets quarterly to look at ways to improve the flow of data to and from the microcomputer environment and the systems it interacts with.

Finally, the standards subcommittee seeks to set standards for the organization in order to achieve economies and efficiencies, and to otherwise make the microcomputer environment more manageable. Working groups will tend to spring up as issues arise pertaining to standardization in one area or another. For instance, a working group on document management standards may be established when it becomes apparent that the current system of storing documents is not appropriate. Other working groups that might arise include operating

	Schedule of Committee Meetings				
	Meeting group				
Month	Monthly	Every 2 months	Every 3 months	Every 6 months	Annually
January	Security Disaster planning Custom programming CAD	Help desk review Technology planning	Communications	Legal issues Preventive maintenance	
February	Security Disaster planning Custom programming CAD	New technology	Routine maintenance	Insurance issues	
March	Security Disaster planning Custom programming CAD	Help desk review Technology planning	Disaster drill	Viral Audit	
April	Security Disaster planning Custom programming CAD	New technology	Communications	Legal liability audit	Insurance audit
May	Security Disaster planning Custom programming CAD	Help desk review Technology planning	Routine maintenance		
June	Security Disaster planning Custom programming CAD	New technology	Disaster drill		

systems standards, custom programming standards, workstation and printer standards, and application software standards (word processing, desktop publishing, etc.).

Depending on its agenda, the standards subcommittee will set various schedules and goals. For example:

- Operating system—done 1990; not due until 1995
- Custom programming—not done yet; schedule monthly
- Hardware—done 1990; due 1993

	Schedule of Committee Meetings (Cont.)				
	Meeting group				
Month	Monthly	Every 2 months	Every 3 months	Every 6 months	Annually
July	Security Disaster planning Custom programming CAD	Help desk review Technology planning	Communications	Preventive maintenance Legal issues	
August	Security Disaster planning Custom programming CAD	New technology		Insurance issues	Power audit
September	Security Disaster planning Custom programming CAD	Help desk review Technology planning	Routine maintenance Disaster drill	Viral audit	
October	Security Disaster planning Custom programming CAD	New technology	Communications	Legal liability audit	
November	Security Disaster planning Custom programming CAD	Help desk review Technology planning			Backup audit
December	Security Disaster planning Custom programming CAD	New technology	Routine maintenance Disaster drill		

- CAD—not done previously; schedule monthly
- Word processing—done 1991; due 1996
- Spreadsheet—done 1992; due 1997
- Database—done 1992; due 1997

The Planning Committee pulls information from all its subcommittees together into a strategic plan, with specific allocations of money and schedules of events. By bringing the goals of the organization together with the findings of the various subcommittees, this group draws the map for accomplishing stated goals with new technology to enhance the environment that exists today.

The chart on pages 40–41 shows how the schedule of committee meetings might look.

Areas of Expertise

"Jack of all trades, master of one." You and your staff can cover a lot of ground by adopting this philosophy. You're getting trade magazines that flood you with the latest technology. Each one probably contains more than one article that you'd like to read in depth, but you don't have the time. Who does? By spreading the responsibility among your staff, and sometimes among interested nontechnical people, you can develop pockets of deeper expertise than you would otherwise have.

The areas of expertise that you need in depth will depend on the latest technologies that are coming out and on what is going on in your industry and in your organization. They may come up in staff meetings, or you may uncover them in phone support logs. You may find that your industry trade magazines are beginning to have articles that drive you. In choosing a champion for any area of expertise, look for willingness and high level of interest. Once you've identified the area expert, let the whole organization know so that people will divert resources and questions to the expert.

In some cases, the area expert should get formal training, though most of the time exposure is more to the point. Learn by being. You can create a self-fulfilling prophecy this way: Once an expert is identified, and people begin turning to the expert for questions, he or she will gain exposure, experience, and eventually in-depth expertise. As people come across articles or other sources of information, they will pass them along to the area expert, who should have file drawer space ready to save the information after reading it.

This is a very informal, low-cost way to develop expertise within the organization—expertise that you and the rest of the organization can draw upon.

To Do

Before you continue, if you haven't done so already, go back to the first two chapters and begin work on the to-do lists. With these preliminaries accomplished, you'll be ready to jump into the fray. Your first job will be to make an inventory of the hardware, software, and people resources that are within your domain.

Part

2

Taking Charge

Chapter 4

Taking Inventory

Where to Begin

There are several reasons for taking a physical inventory when you arrive on the job. One of the first is orientation—"walking the land" is the best way to get an overview of your terrain. Beyond that, the information you collect will be useful to you:

- When you audit your insurance coverage
- When you're preparing your strategic plan for the near and long term
- When you're determining the legality of software stored on machines
- When you're setting standards and troubleshooting problems

In all these cases, you will need to have an up-to-date and reliable source of information regarding the hardware, software, and skills that are available. You're going to inventory your wiring and other connections to help with troubleshooting, and you're going to ==have a list of the skills and interests of people in the organization to help you develop your committees.==

Even if a list of current hardware and software exists, you can't assume it's up to date. Begin with your departmental checklist and take each department in order. Locate the department head's name on your organizational chart and make arrangements with this person to visit the department and spend up to 30 minutes with each machine and 15 minutes with the primary user of that machine.

Skills Inventory

Before you begin taking inventory of the machines, introduce yourself to the primary users and spend a few minutes to find out what problems, concerns, and wishes are highest in their minds. Show them how the service request form works and let them know that you are there to help them solve problems and to find ways of making their jobs easier and more productive. Explain what you're about to do—take an inventory of what is in each machine and do a preventive maintenance checkup.

As you are talking to these people, look for the ones who have the knowledge and temperament to work on the various committees that you will set up. Some committees require people with strong technical capabilities; others call for a management view of operations. Still others merely require a high interest level. During your interviews, take notes on the resources available to you and log the data in a simple database. One person may have skills in several areas you'll want to track. A database will allow you to search quickly for someone with a particular set of skills or combination of attributes. Some of the fields you'll want to track include:

Name

Position and seniority

Phone

Department

Areas of expertise

Skills (best set up as a pick list, to limit the variations in descriptions)

Committee participation (pick list of committees serving on)

Interest areas

Now you're ready to start on the hardware.

Hardware Inventory

Each machine and each printer should be assigned an internal hardware inventory number. This may be a serial number or something as simple as CPU1, CPU2 . . . , and PRN1, PRN2. . . . Your company name and address should appear with the serial number on the inventory label. Fill out an inventory form for each piece of equipment and keep a copy in the machine's workstation folder. Also enter the information into an inventory database for efficient reporting and usage later on.

The CPU inventory form includes the following important information:

1. *CPU number.* Assign a unique ID number to each CPU, possibly the serial number from the manufacturer.
2. *Name.* Often there is a name associated with a computer, even if it is only the Loan Tracking PC or Judy's PC. These informal names can come in handy when identifying a computer within the department. The formal CPU number should be stamped on a label and affixed to a standard place on each CPU so that quick and easy identification can be made for troubleshooting purposes.
3. *Department.* Determine which department this computer belongs to.
4. *Criticality.* Assign the CPU a rating during the criticality analysis.
5. *Primary user and phone.* For each workstation, there should be one person assigned as the primary user. This person takes responsibility for the equipment, software loaded on local hard drives, backups, and other administrative tasks.
6. *Primary use.* What is typically done on the system? Is it a secretarial workstation for word processing and claims processing, or is it an engineering workstation that uses CAD and project management software primarily, along with some spreadsheet applications?
7. *Vendor.* Where was the machine purchased?
8. *Serial number.* The serial number assigned to the equipment by the vendor will be helpful during the warranty period and later if a hardware maintenance contract is adopted. It may also serve as the CPU number, as noted above.
9. *Make and model.* Note the manufacturer and model number of the machine.
10. *Purchase date and purchase order (PO) number.* The date of purchase and PO number will help for warranty and proof-of-purchase tracking.
11. *Warranty terms.* This information will help determine when and whom to call, and what to expect for service. Typically you can expect a 1-year on-site warranty for new computers.
12. *Maintenance vendor.* If there is a hardware maintenance contract, you'll want this information handy.
13. *Processor and BIOS.* This information will help with support and upgrade planning.

CPU Inventory Form	
CPU ID:	Name:
Department:	Criticality:
Primary user:	Phone:
Primary use:	
Vendor:	Serial number:
Make:	Model:
Purchase date:	PO number:
Warranty terms:	
Maintenance vendor:	Number:
Processor and BIOS information:	
Power supply:	
Battery:	
Memory:	
Drives and controller information:	
Monitor and interface card:	
Parallel/serial ports:	
Network interface card:	
Internal modem:	
Other cards:	
Available slots:	
Installation date:	Installed by:
Date of physical inventory:	By:
Change date:	By:
Change description:	

Printer Inventory Form	
Printer ID:	Name:
Department:	Criticality:
Primary user:	Phone:
Primary use:	
Vendor:	Serial number:
Make:	Model:
Purchase date:	PO number:
Warranty terms:	
Maintenance vendor:	Number:
Connected to:	
Shared by:	
Printer-sharing hardware or software used:	
Toner/ribbon/ink information:	
Replacement vendor:	
Font information:	
Installation date:	Installed by:
Date of physical inventory:	By:
Change date:	By:
Change description:	

14. *Power supply and battery.* Use this information to facilitate replacement orders without reopening the machine.
15. *Memory.* Indicate speed, capacity, location, DIP/SIMM, and manufacturer.
16. *Drives and controller.* For hard drives and floppies, note capacity, manufacturer, and type of interface. If you have a mix of high- and low-density drives, consider labeling each drive with the drive designation and capacity (e.g., Drive A: high density). Drive and media incompatibilities waste time and lead to data loss when users fail to understand the ramifications of working with incorrect media. By identifying the drive type clearly, you may prevent some of these problems.
17. *Monitors, modems, and interface card.* Note the manufacturer and model and other pertinent information (including interrupts), as well as software or switch settings. Include the slot size required for cards, and the sizes of any open slots available.
18. *Date of installation.* Indicate when the machine was first set up and who did it.

The CPU inventory form (see page 50) also asks for the inventory date and the date of any change made to the inventory. A new copy should be filled out whenever a change is made. Staple the most recent inventory form to older forms to create a running history of everything that has been done to the machine.

The printer inventory form (see page 51) includes similar but less detailed information.

Filling out the forms will take some time. Get the available information through your on-site inspection. Hold on to any of the forms that can't be fully filled out in order to collect the missing information later. It may be, for instance, that you will have to take all the forms to purchasing in order to get the vendor, PO, and warranty information.

Your First Preventive Maintenance Checkup

You will have to take the hood off each machine in order to get all the information you need regarding the hardware. While you're in there, you can do your first preventive maintenance (PM) checkup, filling out a service report.

Begin by making note of any peculiarities with respect to the environment that the machine is located in. Is it particularly dusty, hot, or humid?

Next, look inside the machine. Is it very clean, reasonably so, or filthy? What you find will determine when you set the next PM date. If

Preventive Maintenance Service Report	
Date:	CPU/printer ID:
Checked by:	Next PM due:
Environment notes:	
Internal status: Vacuum Reseat cards Check cables Check/replace battery (date) Boot disk files match Boot disk directory attached Directory listings attached System startup file listings attached	
Results of review with primary user:	
Identified problems, concerns, questions, and wishes:	
Actions taken:	
Completion date:	Signature:

the machine is clean, an annual PM is all that is necessary. If the machine is filthy, it may require quarterly or even monthly maintenance.

Vacuum out the machine at this point. Shake out the keyboard, reseat any loose cards or chips, and check the cables for exposed wires or loose crimps. Make note of any problems. Check the battery and replace it if necessary. Fill in the replacement date on the PM service report.

At this point the machine can be put back together. Reboot the machine and make sure it starts up. The remainder of your inventory will pertain to software, but you still have a few things to do for the PM checkup. First make sure that the files on the boot disk match the system startup files. If they don't, make a new boot disk. Keep the disk in the workstation folder, readily available and up to date. Make a hardcopy listing of the boot disk files, along with a directory listing of the hard drive. The listings will help you answer three important questions:

1. What software is being kept on the local hard drive?
2. How well organized are the data on the drive?
3. How close to capacity is the drive?

Attach all these listings to the PM service report. Then take a moment to review your findings with the primary user. If there is anything that needs attention immediately, indicate it on the form and put it in the Open Items section of your master planner. If no further action is called for, date and sign the report as complete. Place a copy of this form in the machine's workstation folder. The original should go with you for further analysis.

Keeping Track of It All

A laptop with a database form will help you gather this information directly into a more useful format; otherwise, you'll have to have it keyed in. Several reports will spring from this information over time.

With your first physical inventory completed, you have a much better feel for what's where. However, this information will quickly become obsolete unless you have a way to ensure that it is maintained up to date. One approach is to keep hardware inventory change sheets in the workstation folders. Of course, whoever is responsible for making the changes will need to fill out the change sheets correctly and send them on their way to you. This may not be a problem if you are always the one responsible for approving the purchase of new hardware and software and carrying out the installation. If, on the other hand, there are several parties involved, you will need to develop an alternative plan.

If purchasing does all the acquisitions, you may be able to use this central repository to get notification of new purchases. Unfortunately, with the low cost of PC equipment and software, the purchasing department is often bypassed; the equipment is purchased, and often installed, directly by the department. You may successfully pass an edict that all PC purchases go through you, but you risk being perceived as the PC police.

If nothing else works, a regularly scheduled physical inventory will have to take place. Fortunately, there are inventory tools that will gather most if not all of the data you'll need, and if you are completely networked you can do much of the process without leaving your office. (The downside of the hands-off approach is that you aren't meeting with the users, and you're not picking up clues from the environment. Still, if you're out and about often enough for other reasons, this shouldn't be a drawback.)

Commercial Software Inventory

The object of the commercial software inventory is to determine what commercial software exists out there, who's using it, and who owns it. There are software inventory products available to assist you in this job, and they will quickly pay for themselves in the time they save you. Without an inventory product, you'll have to scan directory listings of each hard drive as well as the server. Depending on the sophistication of the primary user, you may get some assistance in identifying files and thereby locating software. In an organized PC, the menu system will locate the application files, and the data files will be easy to locate in subdirectories. In many systems you may have complete chaos to sift through. Still, this is good feedback that will give you insight into your user community. Now is not the time to set about organizing the mess, but you'll want to make note of the need.

Look at menu systems and check off the files that can be accounted for from the menu. Check out batch files and any other loose .EXE files floating around. For each application you find, you'll need to identify the name and publisher of the package as well as its basic function. Is it a word processor, accounting package, database product, and so on? Also, the version number needs to be updated with upgrades.

The PO number and the date of purchase will probably not be immediately accessible and can be left blank until you conduct a legal liability audit. The same may be true for the license or serial number. At some point, most easily at purchase time, you need to get a copy of the license. Unfortunately, there are no standard license agreements, and each one must be read and understood before the application is put into use. Note the terms on the software inventory form, and keep a copy of the license in a separate central file.

The terms of any support for the product should also be noted. Is an 800 or 900 number provided by the vendor, or has your organization purchased support from some other third party? Note the expiration date and access hours. If applicable, identify the key users of a particular product. The primary user is the person who is working with the product on a day-to-day basis. If there are many, identify the most ap-

Commercial Software Inventory		
Product name:		
Publisher:		
Function:		
Version:	PO number:	Purchase date:
License/serial number:		
License terms:		
Support terms:		
	Name	Phone
Primary users		
Power users		
Password holders		

propriate users. Are there any in-house gurus on the product? These area experts can be a valuable resource.

Finally, who has the keys or password to use this software if access is restricted? It's imprudent to leave only one person with knowledge of a password. On the other hand, security is increasingly compromised with each new key, and with each additional person who has access to a password. The simplest method is to assign one trusted person with the list of all passwords. This person must obviously have very high security clearance and be available most of the time. The systems manager is frequently assigned this role, but it's a heavy security burden to ask any one person to bear. A slightly less risky but more complicated method is to make sure a minimum of two people know any software product's password. In this case, you won't know all the passwords, but you will have a list of who the two (or more) password holders are for each product. If there is a problem, you can quickly find someone who knows.

The information you collect on all these forms will be helpful for conducting your legal liability audit and for other planning later on. It should also give you an idea of the scope and diversity of the programs out there and who the experts are.

Application Inventory

Related to the commercial software inventory is the application inventory. An application is a particular system that a software product is used for. Often it is one and the same as the commercial software prod-

Application Inventory Form		
Application:		
Platform product:		
Description:		
	Name	Phone
Developer		
Primary users		
Power users		
Password holders		
Are there source codes or macros involved?		
What if you were unable to access this program or the data for a day, week, or month?		
What would be the ramifications of losing a day's worth of data?		
What if a week, month, or year was lost?		
How confidential are the data?		
Would this information be valuable to anyone outside the firm?		
Criticality rating:	Security level:	

uct, as in the case of accounting software. The product is an accounting software product, and the application is accounting. Many applications which are built from commercial products need to be identified separately. If your inventory reconciliation system is tracked through a Lotus spreadsheet, then the application should be kept track of beyond the commercial product defined by your spreadsheet.

Any time a commercial product (such as a spreadsheet or database manager) is used to create a custom application in the form of a macro, script, or compiled source code, you'll want to keep track of the different applications developed. The commercial product should be logged in the commercial product inventory. The applications built with them need to be identified and logged using an application inventory form. This doesn't mean that every spreadsheet needs to be categorized, but the ones that are used over and over should be tracked. Ask the questions listed on the form while you are working with the primary user, so you can get a first cut at the criticality and security levels for the application being discussed.

Mapping Your Terrain

By now you're on more solid ground. You know what hardware and software are out there and how they're being used. You've also met the users and are probably developing a feel for the general level of skills and needs that people have. Now let's take a closer look at the layout of the operation and how it all fits together.

Cartography may not have been required in your computer science course, but mapping skills will come in handy now. You may be able to get a blueprint of your office layout from your electrician, building manager, or landlord. If you are lucky, the blueprint will include a cabling diagram. If not, you will need to superimpose your own diagram after consulting with the party responsible for wiring your office. If you don't have access to reliable information, an electrician can do the necessary detective work to uncover the wiring scheme.

If you have access to a blueprint, keep a master and use copies to overlay with specific information. (There are software tools to enable you to keep this information on the computer, which will assist with planning and changes.) You will want to keep track of the wiring scheme and the location of servers, workstations, and printers. You will use this information both for troubleshooting and for planning. If a single blueprint will become too cluttered, break some of the functions out in a second.

To Do

- Set up meetings for first department.
- Develop skills inventory.
- Tag inventory.
- Label floppy drives.
- Conduct initial PM checkup.
- Develop hardware inventory.
- Take commercial software inventory.
- Take application inventory.
- Create wiring map.
- Create hardware map.

Chapter 5

Criticality Analysis

Lady Bug

You've finished taking inventory. You know who's out there and what everyone is doing. Now you need to know more about how critical these functions are to the continuing operation of your organization, and what types of protection they call for. This is the purpose of the criticality analysis.

Imagine you're a firefighter who has just been called to a factory blaze. You notice two separate fires: Flames are leaping from the factory windows, and a small grass fire has just started between the factory and an old warehouse. Children are playing near the warehouse, where you know that highly explosive chemicals have been stored. The factory is empty. To the uninformed eye, your decision to rush right for the grass fire while the factory blazes may seem silly. However, because you are informed, you have set your priorities correctly.

The criticality analysis should be your first order of business after inventory, and little if anything should take you away from this task until it's complete. If it represents a nagging concern to some high-level people in your organization, it should be a loud and continuous wailing in your own head. Any time something else pulls at your attention, remember the nursery rhyme:

> Lady bug, lady bug
> Fly away home
> Your house is on fire
> And your children are gone

Until you have gone through a criticality analysis, your house is at risk.

Systems List

For each function being performed on computers, you need to establish a criticality rating, which will in turn determine how guardedly you protect that function and how much importance you give it strategically. During your inventory, you collected information about the applications that are out there and the primary users' judgment as to their criticality and security implications. Now it's time to put the big picture together, to fill in any of the missing pieces and develop a plan of action.

Begin by generating a preliminary systems list. Some applications may be systems in themselves. For example, your CAD software package is the application and is also synonymous with the drafting system. Other systems will comprise two or more applications. Thus, the order entry system is made up of the order entry software, the inventory software, and the phone system. Systems are the various functions that are carried out using hardware and software, and that depend on one or more components working together. Two or more systems may share an application. The purchasing system depends on access to inventory, as do the order entry system and the shipping system.

Systems need to be analyzed as a whole for their criticality rating, and a high system rating will elevate the ratings of its subcomponents. If the order entry system is given the highest criticality rating, then its components—the phone system, order entry, and inventory—will also take on the highest criticality rating. Inventory would not be considered critical if its rating were based on the purchasing system (which is viewed as less vital), but it remains high because of its connection with the more important order entry process.

Define your systems list with all its subcomponents identified. Make sure that all the applications in your inventory are accounted for. Assign preliminary ratings of these systems on the basis of your albeit sketchy knowledge, and upgrade any components as necessary.

Now you're ready to call together the first meeting of the Security Committee.

First Meeting of the Security Committee

Since this is your first meeting, you'll have some introductions and orientation work to take care of, but you'll want to get to the point of the meeting quickly: to confirm or change the systems list and the criticality ratings that you have assigned.

The committee should review the ratings as a whole. Independently, supervisors may naturally place critical labels on the most important functions within their department. As a group, they will be able to put their departmental functions in perspective. Your job is to get a sensible consensus, without making any one department feel less important because its functions call for a lower criticality rating.

Because this committee is made up of high-level people whose available time is limited, you need to be particularly well prepared for meetings. By doing the legwork yourself, you will speed things along and earn everyone's gratitude. Because speed is critical at this point, you can be forgiven for bulldozing the way. A week before the meeting if possible, distribute a preliminary report to committee members, along with a memo stating the agenda, time, place, and duration of the meeting. Ask them to review these items and to come prepared to discuss any or all of the ratings.

The meeting should then be able to proceed fairly smoothly. Have members run down the list, reach consensus on the ratings, and discuss any of the differences in opinion that exist. If there is a difference in opinion on the appropriateness of a rating, go with the higher rating and move on.

Accessibility

One of the key measures you'll use to determine the criticality rating is accessibility. How mission-critical is this function? Let's say you work for a large mail-order house. The phone order system is by the nature of the business a mission-critical operation. It's easy to predict the disastrous results ensuing from even a minor disruption in computer functioning in this area. So essentially the accessibility rating comes down to this question: How long can we do without it?

As with all the indicators, your own situation may call for a different rating schema, with more or fewer levels. Keep it as simple as possible, and if a particular rating level has no bearing at all, drop it altogether.

Accessibility rating	Description
Critical	Absolutely necessary, 24 hours a day, 7 days a week
High	Must be back up within the day
Basic	Could be down for 5 days without major interruption
Low	Not time-sensitive, easily reproduced, not necessary to recover

Sensitivity

Another indicator of the criticality rating of a function lies in its sensitivity, or security level. How sensitive is this function? What would be considered a threat to the security of the data?

Sensitivity rating	Description
Top secret	Of great value to competitors
Confidential	For small internal group only
Restricted	Access restricted to management levels
Public	Public information

Integrity

Another helpful question to pinpoint the appropriate criticality level relates to integrity: What would be the impact of erroneous information?

Integrity rating	Description
High	Loss of customers; possible legal action
Medium	Low impact on business decisions; other sources will illuminate discrepancies
Low	Not an important source of information

Strategic Links

How does a given function relate to the strategic goals of the company? Perhaps your company has decided to make customer satisfaction a strategic goal for this year with the implementation of rapid response systems to handle customer inquiries. This function will therefore receive stronger emphasis (though perhaps only temporarily).

Functions that have strategic links can simply be marked with an asterisk in the appropriate column of the criticality analysis sheet. You will want to attend to the very high ratings first. And of these priority

Criticality Analysis Sheet				
Function	Accessibility	Security	Integrity	Strategic link

systems, those with a high accessibility rating will be at the top of the heap.

Backup Policies and Procedures

The ratings and ramifications of not having access will help you determine the appropriate backup measures that should be put in place. If some systems are critical to the point where 24-hour accessibility is required, policies and procedures must be developed now to address this need.

Frequent backups with regular off-site rotation will be mandatory for these systems and should be implemented now. The Security Committee needs to know what the alternative choices are and must be given your recommendation as to backup methodologies, frequencies, and tools. Are all systems backed up automatically to tape each night regardless of their security level? Will mirrored drives be used for every system rated above "basic"? Will you want to establish a hot site to carry out operations in the event that your existing site becomes unusable for the critically rated systems?

Once the group has agreed to the steps needed to ensure the accessibility of various rated systems, you can put the appropriate safety nets in place immediately, starting with the most critical systems first.

The final step of the criticality analysis is to schedule the next review date. Priorities change, operations are dropped and added, and methods of protection are improved and made obsolete. Depending on your findings, a review date should be set for from 1 to 3 years.

To Do

- Draw up list of functions.
- Establish initial criticality ratings.
- Establish Security Committee.
- Submit preliminary report to Security Committee.
- Meet to review ratings.
- Submit report on final ratings.

Chapter 6

Disaster Planning

Disaster planning is the first and most important part of disaster prevention and recovery. Even though we cannot eliminate all the potential threats—flood, fire, lightning strikes, bombs—we can, through thoughtful planning, provide layers of protection to minimize the risks.

A Time to Act

Say you're camping in the backwoods with a friend and you come across a man who has been mauled by a grizzly. You know you need to get him to a hospital quickly and you offer to run like hell for help. Fortunately, your friend is a trained emergency medical technician and yells for you instead to take your shirt off, rip it to shreds, and help create a tourniquet to stop the arterial bleeding. You work together and stop the bleeding, get the man into your sleeping bags to help prevent shock, and then take off. If your friend hadn't stopped you, the man would surely have died while you went to get help.

Likewise, upon arriving on the scene as a new systems manager, you need to assess the systems patient for signs of imminent distress. If there are critical systems with no disaster recovery mechanisms in place, you have a life-threatening situation on your hands—one you must take care of immediately. Take an off-site backup now and plan to redo it every week until the more formal plan is in place.

Once you've isolated the critical components (via the criticality analysis) and insulated them from the raw exposure of having absolutely no measure of security (through your immediate off-site backup measures), you can begin to create a more comprehensive and careful disaster recovery plan. This type of planning comes under the aegis of the Security Committee.

The Bigger Picture

The microcomputer systems disaster plan should become part of a larger business disaster plan. If the business has no contingency plans for dealing with a disaster, there's little sense in recovering the computer operations. On the other hand, there is more chance of a disaster affecting the microcomputer system in the form of electrical violence than of the disaster affecting other aspects of business through fire, flood, or earthquake. Hence, it makes more sense to plan for this type of disaster even when other risks are left in the laps of the gods. But if there is a more comprehensive business recovery plan—in some industries one will be required by law—then the systems recovery plan should be an integral part of it.

The primary goal of the disaster recovery plan is to ensure the operational status of vital computer systems. Recovery of less critical systems should be considered in the plan according to their criticality ratings.

In previous meetings of the Security Committee, you have identified and rated the various systems. You've taken immediate steps to protect the critical functions. Your next step is to focus on the disaster recovery plan and its purpose. As a group, discuss the possible risks to system operations, as well as their ramifications to operations and to the business as a whole. There are the obvious natural disasters, as well as those peculiar to computer systems, such as power problems and vandalism. There are the accidental, the intentional, and the incidental. The more disasters you identify, the better prepared you'll be to deal with them. By identifying the possible risks and their impact on operations, you will begin to see what needs to be done in order to restore operational status.

The next order of business is to outline the plan that you hope to develop. Either you can come prepared with your vision of what the plan should look like, and then let others take time to digest it and come up with suggestions, or you can develop the outline as a group. Things will move faster if you ask for consensus on a preconceived plan than if you develop one as a group. However, speed is less important here than thoughtful consideration. If you hand out your ideas, people will be inclined to nod approval without giving much thought to the issues themselves. The best approach might be to have each member come to the meeting with a list of things to be covered in the plan. This way, you will get input from several sources without predisposing people to anyone else's ideas of what should be covered. Then take all these ideas and come up with a comprehensive outline.

Sample Disaster Recovery Plan Outline
I. Overview
   Background information
   Purpose
   The committee
   The plan
II. Systems
   Accessibility ratings defined
      Critical
      High
      Basic
      Low
   Computer systems descriptions
   Criticality analysis
   Implications
III. Backup procedures
   Standard backup procedures
      Systems accessibility rating: critical
      Systems accessibility rating: high
      Systems accessibility rating: basic
      Systems accessibility rating: low
   Off-site storage
      Documentation
      Procedures
      Inventory listings
      Personnel contact list
      Vendor contact list
      Disaster support contact list
      Insurance contacts
IV. Recovery procedures
   Notification—responsibilities and authorities
   Temporary equipment
   Hot-site facilities
   Telecommunications
   Restoration of critical systems
   Restoration of high systems
   Restoration of basic systems
   Damage recovery
V. Audit procedures
   Objectives
   Components
   Schedule
   Responsibilities
   Recovery plan review
   Insurance audit

Working with Systems

The criticality analysis that you made when you started the job will identify the systems upon which the organization depends most heavily. These are the systems that need to be ready for instant recovery and usability. Disaster recovery deals with systems rather than individual files. Access to the latest data files won't get you very far if you don't have the processing system to work with them.

The higher the criticality rating of a system, the more layers of protection should insulate it. For low-rated systems, an off-site backup taken once a month may suffice. For those with a high criticality rating, daily off-sites may be more appropriate, along with mirrored disks, and 24-hour hot-site availability.

Your backup policies and procedures will delineate what types of backups are taken, and audits will ensure that individual files are recoverable. Disaster planning assumes that this level of protection is in place, but goes another step in asking: What happens if the site itself becomes inaccessible? Off-site backup and hot-site management become a key concern.

Off-Site Backups

Where you choose to store your off-site backups will also depend on the level of operational protection you want in place. If you have a hot site, this may be where you'll store the backups. If a more casual approach is acceptable, then make arrangements for a safety-deposit box, an appropriate consulting firm, your lawyer, or a high-level employee. The facility that you choose should have hours and closings that are compatible with your company's. If you choose a bank, your disaster will no doubt occur on some obscure holiday. If you store your off-site tapes with your lawyer, it will happen when he or she is on vacation. Prepare for the worst. Keep at least two sets off-site on the chance that the most current set doesn't work.

When delineating backup procedures for disaster recovery purposes, you may want to state the frequency of backups required for critically rated systems and the method of off-site storage that you'll use.

You'll want to store your recovery plan and any other vital documentation off-site as well. Keep several copies with various people (including yourself) because you never know who will be the first to learn of the disaster. Contact lists will be important, since you should assume that your Rolodex was either on the computer or blown up, burnt up, or drowned along with the electronic equipment. You'll need to get hold of every member of the recovery team, and you'll need to know what their responsibilities are. Know how to reach your vendors, your suppliers, your computer consultants, your lawyers, your press relations firm, and whoever else needs to be on top of this thing. You'll want to have access to your inventory list and your insurance policies. The order of things to happen, the responsibilities of those involved, contingencies—all need to be delineated clearly in your plan.

The Call

So you get a call in the middle of the night. It's your boss, but she sounds different—panicked. The building has burned to the ground. She's across the street in a phone booth. She left home without her copy of the recovery plan. You tell her to hold while you get your plan. It has the necessary phone numbers to call. You tell her you'll start the notification process and then meet her at the phone booth. You call up your off-site storage facility, which delivers your last off-site backup to you in the parking lot of what used to be your main headquarters, what is now a smoldering pile of charred office equipment. Now what?

Can you set up at another location that your office has? Will you need to rent equipment and space? What will you do about wiring and phone systems? Plan from the disaster forward, and then put it down in the recovery procedures. Planning should include everything from the initial phone calls through insurance recovery.

Audit Procedures

Once you've put together your backup and recovery plans, you'll want to test the plans to make sure they work, and to make sure that everyone involved knows how they will work. Unless the procedures are drilled in, people will forget in the panic of the real disaster. Frequent drills are as important to successful recovery as the recovery plan itself.

Each drill can cover a slightly different component of the plan, and the Security Committee can brainstorm on the various scenarios that might unfold. The committee should review the results of the audits and recommend any changes. Finally, the group should review the plan itself on a yearly basis to ensure that it is still valid.

One of the benefits to having a committee involved in this aspect of your job is that it protects you from the temptation to put planning off until it's too late. If you do, when you get that panicked phone call in the middle of the night, you'll have to pray it's just a nightmare.

Insurance Coverage

Insurance coverage is your last resort. Are you properly protected? What are the requirements of your insurance policy for you to collect on lost, stolen, or damaged data in the event that you make a claim? Check it out. In each disaster scenario you test, determine what insurance would have to cover, and then make sure that your policy handles these needs.

Your basic business policy is not enough. Typically, the property covered in this type of policy is limited to the physical components, and claims for damage resulting from power problems may not be covered. Usually a separate policy is needed to cover software, data, and the problems that are peculiar computer liabilities.

One of the most common losses arises from unrecoverable data. The most typical scenario is that data are lost because of a power surge, and the recovery process doesn't work. Either the backup or restore process was faulty or the media were faulty. Perhaps the operational procedures simply weren't carried out properly. The end result is lost data. In this scenario many insurance companies will not cover you, because the data loss was not in fact due to fire, flood, or electrical malfunction, or other covered problems. It was due in the end to a failed backup mechanism, which was not covered. If you think you're paying for this level of protection, then get verification—in writing.

Too often, agents are overly quick to offer you assurance that your insurance coverage is complete. Only later do you discover where the exceptions are. Read the policy yourself, ask questions, and put down the questions and types of coverage scenarios that you expect to be covered by the policy you are considering. Then get written acknowledgment that you are indeed covered. It isn't that your agent is trying to deceive you; it is often a case of your agent's not having a clear understanding of the policy loopholes. When you place a claim with the insurance company, it will be passed by a claims representative (not your agent), who has been admonished from day one that the most heinous sin is to pay an uncovered claim. Your agent may fight for your side, but unsuccessfully in many cases.

Here are the types of coverage you'll need.

Hardware. Look for replacement costs for similar equipment. In an arena as quickly changing as the microcomputer market, you should not look for book value coverage. You will not be covered for normal wear and tear, so you will have to know what the meantime to failure is of your computer or component if you are going to put in a claim for an older component that dies of seemingly natural causes. Remember that lightning spikes can cause damage that doesn't surface for days or weeks. Your claim is going to fly or be rejected on a combination of factors: the circumstance behind the claim and the amount of the claim. The hardest claim will be one which involves both a high dollar settlement and confusing circumstance. If your machine was 5 years old and your hard drive crashed, was it normal wear and tear or the spike you took during last night's storm?

Software. Commercial software is straightforward. If you have custom software, you will have to apply a value to it and insure against its loss. If you are wise enough, however, to recognize its value and insure against its loss, you are probably smart enough to make sure that copies of the source code are kept off-site, in which case the need for insurance is minimal.

Data. Backups are far better protection than insurance. Even if your claim for data loss is covered, you will have to reenter all your data (if you have other sources of it). Still, what is the value of the data? What is the value of the business you stand to lose while you recover?

To Do

- Set up emergency off-site backups now.
- Get a copy of the business recovery plan.
- Schedule meeting with the Security Committee to begin disaster recovery planning.
- Develop outline for microcomputer disaster recovery plan.
- Schedule audits.
- Check insurance policy.

Part 3

The Protective Audits

Chapter 7

Backup Audits

Pay Now or Pay Later

Your disaster recovery plan will audit the recovery process and will therefore entail test backups of critical systems, but these drills are designed to cover only one type of restoration. Far more common will be the recovery of a single file or disk. Daily backup policy and procedures are designed to protect systems against these more common problems, and the backup audits should test these procedures. The audits are designed to uncover and eliminate any holes in the backup process before the need for those backups comes up.

If there is already a policy in place for backups, check it for currency and completeness, and compliance with the disaster recovery plan. It should go beyond the backup methods described in the disaster recovery plan to cover the types of data loss discussed here. If there's nothing in place yet, start developing a comprehensive defense plan.

Sample Backup Policy and Procedures Outline
I. Introduction
   Background information
   Goals
II. Backup Policy and Procedures
   Data types
   Responsibilities
   Backup logs
   Backup tools
   Frequencies

Backup sets
Labeling
Storage
III. Restoration Procedures
Notification
Reports
IV. New Application Procedures
Notification report
V. Backup Audit Procedures
File recovery audit
Backup procedures audit
Full recovery audit
VI. Forms

Having a policy statement that addresses these issues will create consistency throughout the organization. The statement should be distributed to anyone who will be in charge of backups. Keep in mind that many people will not have a solid understanding of the reasons for (and the implications for not) performing backups according to policy. Therefore, begin with an introductory section that describes the reasons for and goals of the organizational policy.

File Types

During your criticality analysis, you developed a rating scheme for the various applications and systems. Even at the file level, however, there are variations in ratings that have implications for the backup procedures used. The disaster recovery plan addresses protection and restoration from a systems or function level; backup policies and procedures deal with data at the file level. There are several types of file classifications that need to be considered in terms of their backup and restoration implications.

Some files have low or no backup requirements. These include commercial application software which can be restored from master floppies and temporary files which serve no long-term purpose, such as .BAKs and some types of correspondence.

Many files have medium-level backup requirements. These are files which would need to be reconstructed, but for which there are other sources to reconstruct them (paper files) and no immediate need to reconstruct them. This category might include large documents, year-end reports, and old data files.

Volatile data that change daily and have a large impact on customer service or on the operational status of the company must be regarded as needing high-level backup protection. The backup procedures for these files should be maintained and audited rigorously. Customer files, accounting files, and inventory records all fit into this category of data.

Even more critical are those files which are not only volatile and important but also unrecoverable. An example is an on-line order entry system in which operators take telephone orders and enter them directly into the computer. These files require the added layer of constant backup protection found with mirrored drives.

Custom application source code is a separate and difficult class of files to deal with. It includes systems developed using high-level languages, spreadsheets, and database managers. These files may remain static for long periods of time, during which they can be classified as having medium-level priority. When changes are being made, however, this priority can shift to high or even critical, depending on the nature and scope of the changes. Source code, therefore, has to be carefully monitored and backed up when revisions are made. Implementation and notification policies regarding new versions of custom software should be defined in custom application development policy, since version control or revision management has an agenda that goes beyond the objectives of backup policy. Nevertheless, it is worth noting these special considerations here. Configuration files are similar, in that backups are necessary only when a change has taken place. However, less fuss needs to be made over these custom files, since they are usually relatively easy to re-create.

Classifying the various files helps to determine which level of backup protection is necessary. When several types of data are stored on a single disk, the highest-level backup needs should usually prevail for the entire disk. Exceptions to this rule can be argued when the amount of critical data is small and the overall disk size is very large. It's better to have one backup strategy to handle the entire disk rather than separate backup procedures to handle the separate types of data. The reason is that, if your backup procedure identifies one or more subsets of the disk rather than the whole disk, you risk omitting data altogether. Over time, as data are moved around, you'll develop totally unprotected pockets of data, and it won't be obvious that anything is being overlooked until you need it. Better to back up the entire disk at the rate called for by the most critical data stored there, using incremental backups so that more static data aren't being needlessly backed up.

Logs and Tools

The people responsible for backups need to know who they are. They need to know what the implications are for failing to back up, and they need to know that regular audits will take place. If any of these things

Backup Log			
Date	Backup set	Initials	Notes

is left unclear, all but the very cautious will play the odds. By making the penalties high, and backup procedures clear and easy, you're more likely to get compliance. Consider assigning the job to one backup administrator, someone solely responsible for taking backups, rather than making professionals responsible for their own backups. This arrangement is easier to manage, more likely to be executed consistently, and more cost-effective overall.

Establish a backup log that indicates who backed up, when, and what backup sets were used. This helps give the responsible person a visual reminder of the backups that need to be done, and it provides an audit tool for you later.

Standardize on your backup software. Use the same version of the same backup utility, and use batch files or macros to automate the process. The software should be set up to verify the backup and to log any errors. The backup administrator is ultimately responsible for noting the successful completion of backups, even if they take place at 3 a.m. In the back of the backup log keep a section for the error log reports and ask the administrator to print it out and initial the report each morning to verify that it has been checked.

Backup media range from floppies to hard drives to tapes, and can be set up for automatic midnight processing or done manually by the administrator each time. All other things being equal, the simpler the mechanism in place the better. All other things being equal, the faster the better, the quicker to restore the better, the more fail-safe the better, the less expensive the better. But each benefit carries a cost, usually in the form of money or speed. Hard-disk backups are quick but expensive. Floppy systems are cheap (or seemingly so) but time-consuming. The bigger the capacity tape you use, the more expensive the system. On the other hand, the system that at first appears to be the most expensive may actually turn out to be the least-cost alternative when the costs of performing backups over the course of an entire year are taken into consideration.

If you are currently backing up with floppies and want to see whether a more expensive system is justified, put a spreadsheet together that shows the hours and labor cost involved in doing daily backups. Calculate the annual cost of performing backups this way, and add that figure to the cost of all the floppy sets. Then compare the total with the cost of a tape system that sits on your server and pulls data up from local drives automatically. The results of the comparison will usually more than justify the move to a more expensive system. If it doesn't, consider the additional cost of having machines idle during backup time, versus the midnight backup.

When, What, and Where

Establish the frequencies and the methods to be used during backups. Should critical data be backed up daily or twice per day? Your policy should state that all disks containing data of a particular level will be backed up at a set frequency. Determine whether full backups will be taken each time, or whether some sets are to be incremental. Your decision will have implications for the number and size of sets and storage methods used.

How are the backup sets to be labeled? If backups are left to users, you will end up with every possible combination of techniques, from leaving disks unlabeled to adhering new labels every day. A reasonable label format for full daily backup tapes might look like this:

```
MON-A
Server #1
Full -
Fastback 1.0
```

```
TUES-A
Server #1
Full -
Fastback 1.0
```

```
┌─────────────────────────┐
│ WED-A                   │
│ Server #1               │
│ Full -                  │
│ Fastback 1.0            │
└─────────────────────────┘
```

.
.
.

```
┌─────────────────────────┐
│ MON-B                   │
│ Server #1               │
│ Full -                  │
│ Fastback 1.0            │
└─────────────────────────┘
┌─────────────────────────┐
│ TUES-B                  │
│ Server #1               │
│ Full -                  │
│ Fastback 1.0            │
└─────────────────────────┘
```

.
.
.

```
┌─────────────────────────┐
│ JANUARY                 │
│ Server #1               │
│ Full -                  │
│ Fastback 1.0            │
└─────────────────────────┘
┌─────────────────────────┐
│ FEBRUARY                │
│ Server #1               │
│ Full -                  │
│ Fastback 1.0            │
└─────────────────────────┘
```

.
.
.

```
┌─────────────────────────┐
│ 1994                    │
│ Server #1               │
│ Full -                  │
│ Fastback 1.0            │
└─────────────────────────┘
```

A similar set for incremental backups might look like this:

MON-A
Server #1
Full -
Fastback 1.0

TUES-A
Server #1
Incremental -
Fastback 1.0

WED-A
Server #1
Incremental -
Fastback 1.0

.
.
.

MON-B
Server #1
Full -
Fastback 1.0

TUES-B
Server #1
Incremental -
Fastback 1.0

.
.
.

JANUARY
Server #1
Full -
Fastback 1.0

FEBRUARY
Server #1
Full -
Fastback 1.0

```
1994
Server #1
Full -
Fastback 1.0
```

The rest of the information—the specific date of the last backup, who backed up, and so on—would be found on the backup log. Policy should also determine where backups are stored. There's no point going to all the trouble of backing up if you can't find the backups when you need them.

The Restoration Process

Having established backup policies, you can be confident that when someone has lost a file it can be recovered. Now you need to consider how the restoration process will be handled. Ideally, when a data file or disk is lost, the user will contact the backup administrator, who will fill out a data loss form. This form serves several purposes simultaneously. It logs the problem so that you can analyze the longer-range implications: If this is the second time that a drive has gone south, do you really want to keep operating with it? Or if this is the tenth time this same person has accidentally deleted important files, do you think it's time for some further training?

If you never learn about the problems, you can't run interference. The data loss form also serves as a live test of the restoration process. A copy of the report should be made for the audit file. Finally, the data loss might suggest a more worrisome problem. The user is likely to be concerned only with restoring the data. You, on the other hand, need to know if there are broader implications to be considered. Is there a viral infection? Has there been a security breach? The data loss form helps bring out these pieces of information.

Another event that has backup implications is an addition or revision in the application systems housed on a particular drive. The obvious reason to learn about these types of changes is that you may need to revise the backup procedures or format. An application notification form (see page 86) will provide you with the information you need.

Data Loss Form	
Date:	CPU:
Restoration requested by:	
Backup administrator:	
Cause of Loss:	
Last backup:	
Restoration notes:	
To prevent future similar losses:	
To ease future restoration:	
Organizational ramifications:	
Sign-off:	CC:

New/Revised Application Notification Form	
Date installed:	Revision:
Installed by:	
Description of application:	

Commercial software used:
  Licensed?
  Standard?	

Customizations:	
Data involved:	
Backup priority:	
Backup method:	
Primary user:	
CPU:	
Sign-off:	CC:

Testing . . . Testing . . .

The first step in your backup audit is to see whether the appropriate level of backup protection has been set up for each function according to its criticality rating. This is a simple matter of scanning the criticality listing and noting discrepancies between the existing backup methods and those prescribed by the disaster recovery plan.

Backups protect you against many types of loss. Each type of disaster has different implications for your backup approach and the audits you'll need to test them.

Whoops: the accidentally deleted file

A file is deleted accidentally. The fix entails getting the most recent backup and restoring just the missing file alone. Because the loss of single files is such a common occurrence, the procedures for restoring them should be easy, available, and tested frequently to ensure that the process works. The audit is fairly straightforward. The auditor requests the latest backup and the backup log. On the restoration trial form, he or she notes the date of the last backup set taken. Three files are taken at random from the live disk and renamed. (These files should not have changed since the last backup.) The three files are then restored from the backup and a file comparison is made between the restored and the renamed files. At this point, the auditor is confirming that backups are being done and logged, and that they are restorable.

Restoration Trial Form	
Date:	CPU:

Sample files—original path and name
  1.
  2.
  3.	

Sample files—new path and name
  1.
  2.
  3.	

Backup software and procedure	
Restoration procedure	

Comparison of files
  1.
  2.
  3.	

Notes:	
Sign-off:	CC:

Damned spot: damaged areas on the disk

When portions of the disk are damaged, the loss of data may not be immediately obvious. During a backup or other copy procedure, the user may find that a certain file is sitting on a bad spot on the disk and is damaged to one degree or another. There are tools that can help to recover the data, depending on the nature of the problem, but the best protection is the most recent backup. Rename the now-bad data something like .BAD so that the spot on the disk is not reused. (You may want to use more sophisticated tools if the physical damage is limited to a small area and the current file size is large.) Then restore the last backup copy of the file. Since most backup programs will indicate when they have trouble reading or writing, the most recent backup copy should be good. This is the main reason for using the verification pass if it is an option on your backup. While it slows down the backup process, it will catch these types of anomalies. During the audit, verify that the setup options of the backup software include a verification pass.

All backup methods should be examined for their efficiency as well as their effectiveness. Backups done manually by floppy become not only prone to problems as the number of floppies increase but also expensive when labor is taken into consideration. Sometimes, a COPY command to a floppy is adequate. At other times, a central backup tape with the ability to upload and back up local drives is more appropriate. During the audit, you'll get information on the time it takes to do backups as well as the methods being used. This information will help you revise old backup methods when they become untenable.

Something is rotten: data corruption

Data corruption can happen for a variety of reasons. If there is no physical damage to the disk, your backup software has no way of knowing that the data are not valid. Thus, it is harder to catch the corruption immediately, and if the error is not uncovered during normal daily usage, it can go on for weeks or months without detection. This is the primary reason for having several sets of backups. The audit should not only test the physical backups but look at the schedule of backups and the number of backup sets maintained. Perhaps annual, quarterly, monthly, weekly, and daily backups are taken. How long is each set kept before it is rotated? Policy might specify, for instance, that the annual backups are kept for 5 years; the monthlies are rotated yearly, the weeklies rotated monthly, and the dailies rotated weekly. Your audit might well uncover that even though daily backups are being taken, the same backup tape is being used over and over. The more distinct sets that are saved, the greater your chance of recovering from a data corruption problem that will span back through several backup sets.

If there are several backup sets, then labeling and storage become important, because you'll have to be able to locate and identify the sets you need in the event of this type of failure. A log will help identify when various sets were last used, who performed the backup, and where the sets were stored. Your audit should take a look at these matters.

A funny thing happened: datapath failure

Your data are fine but something is wrong along the read/write path. It may be as simple as dirty read heads on a floppy drive, or it may be a bad I/O card. By eliminating the problem, you will regain access. Often, though, you will not be able to boot the system itself, especially if there is a problem with the I/O path. A boot disk with copies not only of the operating system but of other configuration files as well can assist you when you find yourself in this dilemma. Each machine, therefore, should have a boot disk available. Your audit will verify this. Whenever you do a preventive maintenance checkup, you should examine the boot disk as well.

Crash: media failure

Your disk is bad. Assuming that you cannot recover the data through software utilities or data recovery services, your only option is to restore the complete system from backup onto another drive. Your most recent backup will work.

If there are serious ramifications to losing even a small amount of data, for even a small amount of time, then disk mirroring is probably called for. Even if one disk fails, the other will be available immediately.

The file recovery audit should be run fairly frequently—two to four times per year. A second audit of the procedures should be done once every year or two, unless personnel turnover or poor audit results call for a higher frequency. This backup procedures audit (see page 90) should examine the resources, tools, and automation processes used to facilitate backups.

Full Disk Recovery

The final audit that needs to be performed is full disk recovery. This audit covers the inevitable nightmare come true: The CFO comes into the office early one morning to work on the year-end report due at the board meeting that day. Logging into the network, the CFO receives an ominous message: "Unable to locate server." The drive has gone south.

Backup Procedures Audit			
Date:			CPU:
Auditor:			Last audit:
Primary user:			Phone:
Attach copy of backup log:		Up to date?	
Frequency adequate?			
Backup sets used:			Rotation:
Adequate backup set labeling:			Storage:

Is verification set on?
 	
Boot disk availability?
Do system files match?
 	
What resources are used for backups now?
    Time
    Media
 	
What tools are used for backup?
Version?
 	
What automation processes facilitate the backup?
 	
Test file recovery results:
 	
Live file recovery results:			

Implications:			
Recommendations:			
Next scheduled audit:			
Sign-off:			CC:

The CFO goes through the roof. You wish you'd called in sick (certainly you're feeling ill). Barring some problem with your backup last night, you assure the CFO, nothing will be lost but a little time. Your full recovery audit will ensure that there are no surprises waiting for you at this critical point in your career.

A compatible machine needs to be used for the full disk recovery, and this often means renting a machine for the day. If you have several machines, rent the largest-capacity machine and plan to test several machines during the day. To test the recovery process, simply try to restore the system to the temporary machine. Barring any problems with the restoration, bring the temporary system up and run several applications. This audit is primarily designed to catch the various "gotchas" involved in restoring the whole system. The most common problems will revolve around restoring the operating system and the necessary restore programs to the temporary machine. Full recovery is the most expensive and time-consuming of the audits. However, since this type of failure is also the most devastating, it needs to be done annually at a minimum.

The element of surprise

Full backup restoration can take time and will require cooperation and coordination with the primary user. For the other audits, it is more instructional not to forewarn the target user. After all, the purpose of the audit is to simulate the problem event. These kinds of surprises, however, are often seen as aggressively hostile—and they are in that they seek out failure and weakness in others. If users have grown to know you and love you, because of all the happy, helpful problem-solving expertise you have provided, and if you go about this part of your job in a low-key and inoffensive way, then you may succeed in not making enemies. However, if you're concerned about keeping the peace, hire outside auditors. They can take the heat, leaving you to help the user comply.

The results

The information gathered in the audit forms can be stored in a database to help with scheduling and generating reports. After completing your first round of backup audits for the company, you may realize the need to change policy or procedures. Present your findings to the Security Committee so adjustments in policy can be made.

You will also find through your audits that there are wide variations in the care that various departments or people take with respect to backups. Reports on these findings need to find their way into the hands of people who can make the scofflaws come around. Depending on the nature of the problems identified, additional follow-up audits should be scheduled, and follow-up reports issued.

To Do

- Generate backup policy and procedures.
- Identify backup administrator.
- Set up restoration notification process.
- Set up application notification process.
- Set up file recovery audit schedule.
- Set up backup procedures audit schedule.
- Set up full recovery audit schedule.

Chapter

8

Viral Protection

The Big Scare

The scariest thing about viruses is that you don't usually know you're infected until it's too late. While we can talk about protection, detection, and recovery, we are to some degree still whistling in the dark. There are no completely safe systems in existence today, and each form of precaution carries some degree of inconvenience. As a result, most of us settle for some middle-of-the-road mode of coverage that doesn't alleviate our worst nightmares.

Backups, the bottom-line defense against attack, may be only as good as your oldest backup. Depending on the type of backup you use, and the type of virus you encounter, your backed-up data could easily be in jeopardy as well. Rabid paranoia is justifiable considering the value of what is at risk. But what's a rational systems manager to do?

First, you need to understand the nature of *viruses*—the catchall term for an entire species of programs known more correctly as "malignant software." Viruses are a particularly malicious breed in that they are capable reproducing themselves. The more passive strains of malignant software rely on your COPY command to procreate. The more aggressive strains (true viruses) can infect and damage more machines faster. While the different categories help to clarify malignant software, they are all subsets or evolutionary developments of the same genre and bear more similarities than differences.

The self-replicating nature of the software virus is simply the next level of sophistication in the development of software for destructive purposes. Even the prankster variety is ultimately destructive. While such strains may not do any physical damage, they destroy confidence. How would you feel if, upon turning on your computer one morning, you got this announcement: "Your computer is stoned! Please contact your congressional representative to legalize marijuana." Nothing happens to your data, so why worry? It's the same creepy feeling you'd get if you came home from work one day to find this note left on your kitchen table by some stranger: "Just stopped in to watch some TV. Thanks." It's a violation of trust. And if we cannot operate in an environment of trust, we can't share data, which is much of what computers are all about. So there is no such thing as a harmless virus.

On the other hand, some viral strains truly are destructive. They can destroy all the data on your hard drive, bring a network to its knees, even blow up a monitor.

Strains of Malignant Software

What are the most common forms of malignant software? There are *Trojan horses,* which, like the hollow wooden statue given by the ancient Greeks to the Trojans, look benign but contain the tools for destruction. Whoever said "Never look a gift horse in the mouth" wasn't talking about shareware. And when the gift comes in the form of free software, be especially careful. Scan it with a viral detection package before you install it. Trojan horses don't usually tell you what they've done until they've done it. Then, adding insult to injury, they're likely to deliver some defiant message along the lines described above.

Worms are named for snakelike performance in all its literary symbolism. A worm is a low-life incarnate, stealthily slipping through your data, in memory and on disk, flipping bits. Its damage ranges from bad to worse: Bad is when all your data have been corrupted. Worse is when the worm effects subtle enough changes that it invalidates the integrity of your data, without leaving a trace. In this nightmarish scenario, you might go on operating indefinitely with (and backing up) corrupt data.

A *logic bomb* is code that is set to execute upon the existence of a particular set of circumstances. These are often implanted by in-house programmers seeking revenge. One manufacturer of hospital products fired its systems manager and called in consultants to take over the systems management functions. Without any sophisticated tools, the consultants found a program called RETIRE that had been written by the old systems manager. Knowing that his days were numbered, the manager had set up this early retirement plan, which he hoped to activate if he was fired. Because he wasn't given the opportunity to set off his bomb, it lay there waiting.

Wisely, before firing the manager, the client had unplugged all the terminals and changed the locks on the doors, the dial-in phone number, and the passwords on the system. But the bomb was still lying there like an old mine waiting to be tripped over. Had anyone run the program to see what it did, it would have displayed an unprintable message that began with "I would like to convey with the strongest of sentiments" while it deleted all the files on the hard drive and reformatted. Being the sort of guy he was, the old manager never did backups, and had he run this piece of inelegant code the company would have had a disaster on its hands.

The level of sophistication found in malignant software programs has gone well beyond the simple instructions found in RETIRE. Not only can some of these programs erase their own paths, leaving little or no trace of their violating nature, but they can do their dirty work upon examination as well as execution, and are capable of destroying hardware as well as data. Smart malignant software will alter the attributes of a system command file, alter unused portions of the code, and then change the attributes and data back to their previous status, leaving no change in file size.

If you know the signatures of the various existing viruses, you can more quickly identify and eradicate them from your system. Any volume you find labeled BRAIN is likely infected by the *Pakistani brain virus,* which will copy itself onto all bootable disks inserted into an infected computer. Like others of its ilk, the Pakistani brain virus hangs out in the boot sector of the disk. Other viruses are inserted into the code of operating system functions which are found on all or most systems, thus ensuring the presence of a host on each new machine. Some stand boldly alone, perhaps hidden, perhaps asking for attention. An example is the READ.ME file with embedded escape sequences that don't display on the screen but direct ANSI.SYS to execute an undesirable command string.

By staying up to date on the development of new viruses, you will stay abreast of the latest protective measures, as well as new viral signatures that may give you warning of impending disaster or at least allow you after the fact to identify the source which will help you eradicate it.

Viral protection software companies are constantly monitoring state-of-the-art malignant software, and each tries to outfox the other. Each package will offer one or more programs designed to protect against, identify, and eliminate certain strains.

Defensive Policies and Procedures

As the systems manager, you want to establish your defensive policies and procedures to minimize the risk your computer systems face from these aggressive foes. You will want to select an antiviral program as your standard and begin your viral audit for each CPU in your inventory. When investigating each of the packages, you will want to see how it performs on various levels:

- How does it protect against boot disk infections?
- Will it disallow the modification of certain software?
- Will it help with identifying ANSI.SYS remapping?
- What specific viruses will it guard against?

Remember too that this program will come with monthly, quarterly, or annual updates, and you will want to subscribe to these updates and keep everyone current.

There are some obvious dos and don'ts. Scan floppies before you use them. Whenever possible, write-protect floppies so that viruses can't be spread through them. If you have viral protection that needs to be apprised of the original size and attributes of software for later comparison, the time to run the software is immediately after installing the shrink-wrapped product. While recent developments have shown that even shrink-wrap doesn't guarantee safe data transfer, it certainly reduces the number of problems you're likely to introduce. Run virus detection scans before, not after, backups to reduce the likelihood of spreading the infection to your backups.

Do let users know what to be on the lookout for. They should be instructed to alert you to any suspicious malfunctioning or odd behavior. Users should also be advised against bringing in floppies from the outside, and given procedures for certifying any disks that do come in. Still, like the person who chooses to live out life in a closet to avoid the many possible disasters lurking in today's dangerous world, a totally isolated machine has limited value. E-mail systems and other communications software are designed to share data and knowledge and cannot be obviated for the sake of reducing risks.

In the Event of an Attack

What you will do in the event of a virus attack depends on the circumstances. Do you know the type of virus that got you? If so, then you will know its manifestations and more easily how to eradicate it. You may then be able to simply run an antiviral utility for that virus, restore your data from backup, and go about your business. If you don't know what hit you, you are in for a long and brutal war.

What happened to set the thing off? Did someone type something, run something, or just boot up the machine on the wrong day? If you know what activated the virus, you can more easily track it to its source. Until you know what you're dealing with, you won't know best how to recover. You can make matters worse by proceeding blindly. What if you are infected with a virus that not only attacked a month-end procedure and triggered the reformatting of your local hard drive, but also infects the restore program of your backup so that upon execution it erases itself and the server? Maximum mayhem is the chief aim of the idiot who wrote this piece of code, so expect the worst and plan for it.

Protecting the integrity of your backup and restore software becomes paramount, and certainly a closely monitored backup schedule is equally imperative. If you are dealing with a date-activated virus, such as the Michelangelo strain, you can usually avoid bringing up the system with that date after detection and until eradication.

How do you get rid of a bug that's infested your system? Depending on the nature of the infection, you may have to go so far as to reformat the drive, restore the boot sector (some viral protection software will keep a read-only copy of the boot disk for you), or restore one of the operating system programs or applications. These programs are designed to be tricky and they are designed to reproduce, so take care to see that you are completely free of them. There are known strains which can infect CMOS RAM and remain resident even after the computer is turned off. And remember that any full backups that you have run have backed up the malignant software as well, so you will need to ensure that only the data are restored and not the infection.

Remember, it takes only one floppy with an active virus left on it to infect the company all over again. When you've been hit, you'll have to inspect every floppy that is currently in circulation. Upon a successful scan with the antiviral software, mark each floppy with a dated sticker. Continue to check hard drives frequently, watching for any signs of reinfection.

You may choose a TSR version of an antiviral utility that will run continuously and monitor all access and changes to programs and data. Or you may use a program that needs to be rerun on occasion to perform the comparisons that are the basis for its protection. If you run the latter, set the schedule according to the critical rating of the machine and make sure there is a mechanism in place to ensure that it is run regularly. Antiviral programs don't take long to execute, so consider modifying the autoexec to run a program on startup. Keep in mind, however, that viruses are being discovered daily. It stands to reason that if viral-scanning disks have to continue to grow to incorporate the detection and restoration software necessary to handle each new virus, there will come a day in the not too distant future when these programs will take hours to run through their litany of programs. What will we do then?

Again, make sure you're signed up to receive updates to your viral protection software automatically. If you don't, you may run an old version of your viral detection utility and, finding that it detected nothing, think you are protected.

To Do

- Evaluate viral protection software.
- Choose a standard program and review it with the Security Committee.
- Set standards for scanning according to the security levels of various functions.
- Install viral protection software everywhere.
- Set up dates for random audits.
- Set date for review of software and plan.

Chapter 9

Legal Audits

Microcomputer usage carries with it certain legal responsibilities. As the microcomputer manager, you need to be aware of the legal issues. You can leave the wording of legal contracts and such to your legal department, but you will still need to know what issues may create a need for legal services.

Piracy

The most common legal issue for any large microcomputer installation today is piracy. In the United States, software piracy is now regarded as a federal crime and is subject to severe penalties. The minimum penalty calls for up to 1 year in prison and a fine of up to $25,000 for any case of illegally copying or distributing software.

There is some gray area in determining what constitutes piracy, but the basic tenets are fairly clear:

- Backup and archive copies are OK.
- Copies of single-user licenses cannot be run simultaneously on two separate machines or put on a network file server for sharing.
- You cannot rent, lease, or lend commercial software to third parties without the express consent of the software vendor.
- In most cases you may transfer your license of a commercial software product to another party, as long as you relinquish your rights and all copies.
- A license upgrade (where your initial license entitles you to upgrade at a lower cost) signifies an addendum to the original license, not an

additional license. You cannot give away (or sell) the earlier version of an upgraded program.

The blurriest area pertains to the "single license for a single machine" concept. At first glance, this may seem straightforward, if overly burdensome: one machine, one copy. But no court will find you guilty if you move your software to a second machine because the machine you originally installed the software on breaks down. So the concept, strictly speaking, is not one license, one machine. It is more like one license, one user. But again, no judge will find you guilty if you have two part-time secretaries—one on Monday, Wednesday, and Friday, and the other on Tuesday and Thursday—who work on the same machine but never on the same day. So technically speaking a single license is not limited to a single user.

Suppose, however, that your business expands and you have both secretaries working 5 days a week. If one copies the word-processing program to another machine, you are culpable. What if you know for a fact that, even though each secretary is now full time, they do their word processing on separate days and use the two copies only for convenience, since they work in different areas of the department? What about the user who wants a copy to continue working at home? If you removed your office copy before the employee went on leave, and the employee removed his or her home copy upon returning, you would probably not be found in breach of contract. Also, what if the program is loaded on two machines but being used only on one? These are the shady areas, and penalties are likely to reflect the intent and extent of the violations as well as the mere fact of a problem. You may get an understanding judge. Then again you could be fined and sent to jail.

The bigger the numbers you're dealing with, the more likely you are to be audited and the bigger the penalty will be. The Software Publishers Association (SPA) has an 800 number for anyone (such as a disgruntled employee) to report copyright violations, and will file lawsuits against companies as well as individuals.

OK, so you know the law, but you don't control what gets copied onto individual PCs. The first step is to develop your corporate policy regarding the use of microcomputer software. The following sample policy is suggested by the SPA:

> 1. (Company/Agency) licenses the use of computer software from a variety of outside companies. (Company/Agency) does not own this software or its related documentation and, unless authorized by the software developer, does not have the right to reproduce it.
>
> 2. With regard to use on local area networks or on multiple machines, (Company/Agency) employees shall use the software only in accordance with the license agreement.

3. Company/Agency) employees learning of any misuse of software or related documentation within the company shall notify the department manager of (Company's/Agency's) legal counsel.

4. According to the U.S. Copyright Law, persons involved in the illegal reproduction of software can be subject to civil damages of as much as $50,000, and criminal penalties, including fines and imprisonment. (Company/Agency) does not condone the illegal duplication of software. (Company/Agency) employees who make, acquire, or use unauthorized copies of computer software shall be disciplined as appropriate under the circumstances. Such discipline may include termination.

I am fully aware of the software use policies of (Company/Agency) and agree to uphold those policies.

_____
Employee Signature and Date

According to the SPA, "when companies sign a policy statement stating their intention to ensure employee compliance with copyright regulations, the risk of software piracy is reduced." When employees are required to sign such a statement, their own inclination to copy software without giving it a second thought is also reduced.

The Initial Audit

Your next step is to set a date for your initial audit. In preparation, you will have to pull together the records of all your software purchases and copies of the license agreements. (For future audits, a procedural instruction should be given to purchasing to send you copies of purchase orders and license agreements along with registration cards.) Whether you use an existing inventory software product or devise your own database, you'll want to facilitate the cross-referencing of purchase orders, licenses, and physical copies.

A meeting of department heads, your legal counsel, and senior management representatives should be called so that the appropriate course of action can be determined. At the meeting, explain how the audit will transpire and get discussion going on the key issues.

One major question is whether employees will be notified. If employees are not notified of the date of the audit, they should be notified of the existence of the audit structure and the fact that audits will transpire over the course of the year. Notification will raise employees' expectations and make them aware that the organization takes its responsibility seriously. The knowledge that an audit will happen at some unknown, but definite point in the future will eliminate many violations by itself.

The SPA provides the following suggested memorandum to employees:

TO: (Specify Distribution)
FROM: (Senior Management Official)
SUBJECT: PC Software and the Federal Copyright Act
DATE: (Insert)

The purpose of this memorandum is to remind you of the Company policy concerning software duplication. Any duplication of licensed software, except for backup or archival purposes, is a violation of the Federal Copyright Act. Each software program, such as Lotus 123 or WordPerfect, that the Company licenses is to be used on only one microcomputer at a time. If the microcomputer has a program loaded on its hard disk, then that particular program, which is serially numbered, should not be loaded on any other hard disk. This means that if a department has 10 microcomputers with Lotus 123 installed on each, then that department should also have 10 sets of original documentation and system disks.

All microcomputers purchased by the company are being supplied with newly licensed copies of (insert name(s) of software program(s)) installed on them. (Insert name of employee) is responsible for ensuring that each program is properly registered with the software publisher.

The Company will not tolerate any employee making unauthorized copies of software. Any employee found copying software other than for backup purposes is subject to termination from the Company. Any employee giving software to any outside third party, including clients or customers, is also subject to termination. (If you want to use software licensed by the Company at home, you must consult with (insert name of employee) before removing the system disks from the premises.) This policy may seem harsh, but unless we enforce a strict policy on software use, the Company will be exposed to serious legal liability.

(Insert name of employee) will be visiting the departments over the next week to inventory hard disks and to ascertain that original documentation and system disks exist for each copy of a software product resident on a hard disk. If documentation and/or disks are not present, then they will be ordered and charged to that office. Please organize your documentation and system disks for (insert name of employee)'s review.

If you have any questions, please do not hesitate to contact me.

This memo gives the employee notice that the audit will occur within a week. While the unscrupulous user may take this opportunity to back up and unload pirated software before the audit, other employees will appreciate having time to get the necessary documentation in order.

Determine who should do the audit. This may be your job, or you may want to consider using an outside firm, particularly if you think the job may become unpleasant. Better to let an outside firm play the role of computer cop, leaving your positive relationship with people intact.

What if unauthorized software is discovered? The SPA suggests that finding unauthorized copies within a department is tacit approval to purchase (and charge) for that software. This may be the appropriate course of action, or unauthorized copies of software can simply be removed. Deleting unauthorized software is a drastic step, particularly if the software is being used heavily. People will say they weren't aware that a product was unauthorized, and there may be an explanation. Rather than taking any immediate or sweeping action, it may be more desirable to record the unauthorized copies, and then on a case-by-case basis determine the source of the violation and the actions to be taken.

The Audit Report

What information should go into the audit report? Include a list of unauthorized programs and where they were found, who is responsible for the violation, the response to the violation, the actions taken (including any disciplinary measures), and finally the date for the next audit. If the organization comes out clean, an annual audit should be

Software Copyright Violation Form	
Software product:	License number:
CPU number:	Responsible person:
Reason for violation:	
Record of previous violations:	
Action taken:	
Disciplinary action recommended:	
Date	Auditor:

adequate. If there are numerous violations the next (surprise) audit should be scheduled much sooner. Summarize any unauthorized usage on a software copyright violation form (see page 103). Keep a copy of this form in the employee's file as well as in a central location. During follow-up audits, check for repeat offenses, which need to be handled more severely.

Custom Software

When an employee develops custom software for your organization, the organization typically retains the rights to the code. Unless otherwise specified in contracts with outside vendors, rights to the code remain with the contractor. This arrangement carries two important implications: While the contracting party (your organization) retains the rights to use the contracted software, it cannot market the delivered product unless specified in the contract. By the same token, the contractor has the right to market the code to other, possibly competing parties, unless specifically barred from doing so in the contract.

In a custom software development contract, you will want to enumerate several items:

- What are the deliverables?
- What functionality is required?
- What documentation and training are included in the contract?
- What are the systems requirements with respect to security, response time, and other factors?

Keep in mind that a contract does not amount to, and may get in the way of, trust between you and a vendor—trust that will be needed for any successful implementation of a product. The cost of specifying each and every possible contingency and deliverable will be extremely expensive and time-consuming, and probably in the end lacking. It is often better to have trust, and to work on small increments that can be used and tested along the way. Any breach of trust that occurs along the way can be settled by the termination of further work, without undue exposure on either side.

This is not to say that expectations should not be set in writing before work begins, or that plans and milestones should not exist. However, if trust is replaced by contracts, the relationship will rarely be happy, and the results will rarely be satisfactory. In the event that a contract is needed, look to existing templates for software development. Your legal counsel will be able to flesh out the finishing touches.

Viral infections

You will not be found legally guilty if your client's or customer's computer is infected with a virus that came from your company's disks, as long as the infection was unknown to you and your access to the system was authorized. However, caution is always the rule. In the future, there will no doubt be negligence cases brought to trial alleging that sophisticated parties did not do enough to ensure that distributed software or disks were uncontaminated.

If your organization distributes data in the form of disks, establish a procedure for checking each disk before it is shipped. The shipping department can be alerted to check off an indicator on the disk itself before shipment. Consider setting up a central quality control desk to which all disks are sent for examination before going out the door. Issue a virus check (VC) stamp indicating that a disk has been checked. Even without the legal implications, for the sake of client relations you will want to eliminate the possibility of participating in the spread of an infection.

Service contracts

When entering into service contracts with outside vendors, you will want to establish first of all what the service provider is required to provide. Does the contract specify a specific outcome or product, or does it cover an effort only, in terms of work and skill level? If an outcome is not spelled out, the courts are likely to presume "effort only" should a dispute arise. Any qualitative measurements can help define the contract as outcome-oriented.

A word about timeliness: Even if your contract with a software developer specifies deadlines, requires adherence to schedules, and delineates specific penalties for missed dates, you will not necessarily be excused from payment obligations in the event that these deadlines are not met. With respect to service contracts, it is understood that even with diligent performance, in both the planning and the execution stages, deadlines are necessarily arbitrary, and the required time to complete a task cannot be predicted with any substantial accuracy. Normally you will be required to fulfill your payment obligations and then seek damages if any can be tacked to the delay.

Some specific issues that should be covered in a service contract include:

- Data integrity
- Timeliness or services and reports

- System availability
- Deliverables during the course of the contract
- Completion of the contract

The specifics will depend on the nature of the service itself.

Fraud

In your role as systems manager, you may come across what you believe to be a case of fraud, simply because computers are often complicit in acts of fraud. When you are aware of the symptoms, contact your legal counsel for specific actions that you should take.

> Fraud requires proof of a party's (1) knowing (2) misrepresentation of a (3) material fact made with the (4) intent to deceive (5) that is in fact justifiably relied on by the other party to its detriment.[1]

Realize you'll have to have your ducks in line to prove such a claim, and you'd also better have proof of damages sufficient to warrant the ensuing legal fees.

Unauthorized Access

Unauthorized access usually involves two wrongful acts:

> The fundamental or underlying criminal act involved in most computer crime statutes is unauthorized access to or use of a computer system. Often, the criminal penalty attaches more severely to acts involving access to the system with the intent to accomplish an additional defined criminal objective, such as theft of funds, embezzlement, destruction of data, or the like.[2]

A charge of this type will be much more defensible if you have a protective scheme in place which has been violated. Catching the unauthorized user and proving unauthorized access can be very difficult, but if you suspect a snoop, or worse, then it's time to don your sleuth's cap and set a trap.

Privacy is not only a matter of common courtesy, but an individual right. The right to privacy of information should be maintained and protected whenever sensitive information is stored on microcomputers.

---

[1] Raymond T. Nimmer, *The Law of Computer Technology,* Warren Gorham Lamont, Boston, Ma., 1992, p. 10.2.

[2] Raymond T. Nimmer, *The Law of Computer Technology,* Warren Gorham Lamont, Boston, Ma., 1992, p. 12.12.

The more sensitive the data, the more care that should be taken when copying or allowing access to data. While the law may find the perpetrator guilty of illegal access, you too may be culpable if you haven't provided the proper level of protection for sensitive information.

Legal Issues Subcommittee

The best way to ensure that piracy, fraud, and other matters are given the right level of attention on a regular basis is to establish a legal issues subcommittee of the Security Committee, to review and monitor policy and procedures that affect the legal standing of the organization's systems. To ensure that communications links are bidirectional, this group should include your legal counsel as well as representatives from each department. The scheduling of these meetings will vary over time, probably being more frequent initially and then less so. The group should meet semiannually, at any rate, to revisit the issues and determine whether revisions in the law, or internal changes, should be reflected in updated policies. Increased used of laptops, for instance, will require thought and planning to ensure that software taken home by employees is properly accounted for.

To Do

- Establish corporate policy regarding piracy.
- Set up annual distribution of policy to all employees.
- Schedule audit.
- Call first meeting of legal issues subcommittee.
- Review results of audit, determine corrective action, and schedule follow-up audit.
- Develop diskette distribution policy and procedures.

Chapter 10

Access Audits

The ostrich approach has never worked. If you have data worth protecting, you've got to look at the risks head on. Bury your head in the sand, and sooner or later someone will trespass. By learning how to set appropriate security levels, and how to perform an unauthorized-access audit, you can minimize the threat that this risk poses.

Motives

Curiosity, greed, revenge... The reasons people access computer files they're not supposed to are the same reasons people do anything they shouldn't. By exploring the motivations for as well as the mechanisms by which unauthorized access occurs, you'll expand your understanding and thereby increase your ability to protect. What are the reasons that users access data which were not intended for them?

Curiosity is probably the most common cause behind the low-level security breach. If you put the company's payroll file in a public directory called \PAYROLL, how many employees do you think would not take a peek? In situations like this, the peekers could probably argue a case for entrapment. Obviously, we need to avoid leading others into temptation, coworkers who would otherwise mind their own business. Even if none of your coworkers would ever stoop to snoop, it may be possible for the innocent user to stumble into the wrong data unintentionally and become the unwitting recipient of unauthorized information. It's like leaving the door to a secure area unlocked: sooner or later someone will stumble in thinking it's the public rest room or the broom closet. These types of violations are usually minor in consequence, but since prevention is easy (appropriate network security levels), they should not come up as often as they do.

Greed is a common enough motivator in the more serious breaches. Leave something of value around long enough, and someone will eventually walk away with it (or a copy of it). As with the decision to lock your car door when you run into a store, you take into consideration many things: What kind of neighborhood am I in? I'm less likely to lock my car in my home town than I am when I go to the city. Security is less of a problem with a small self-contained network than with an enterprise WAN spanning cities or countries. How long will I be gone for? What can happen in 10 minutes, right? What is there of value to steal? I know that leaving my purse on the seat is asking for trouble, so I hide it. Likewise the payroll data. That battered-up book written and autographed by Mark Twain that I found at a tag sale—it doesn't look important, but I know it is, so I hide it and lock my car doors, even though I'm in my home town. Likewise the patent information. Though the risk of any problem is low, I know I'll kick myself if I fail to take the extra precautions and then lose my find.

Oddly enough, many companies that are otherwise fairly conservative in their risk-taking behavior all but overlook a lackadaisical approach to leaving valuable data lying about. Like the hometown hick visiting the big city, these companies may be unpleasantly surprised to find out that there are sophisticated data thieves ready to snatch up unprotected data. You, as the principal guard at the gates, need to be more sophisticated than the other users, and to assume that the "other guy" has the wherewithal and the lack of morals to come after your company's data. And unpleasant as it is to consider, outsiders aren't the only potential perps. Embezzling funds will always be a high-risk, high-reward endeavor for insiders with the skills, access, and appropriate greed factor.

Challenge is a more adolescent motive—or a more sublime one, depending on whom you ask. To the hacker who trespasses electronically, any security measures represent an intellectual challenge. Hackers break it because it is there. But they refuse to see the longer and wider implications of their pursuits. Like the self-centered adolescents they frequently are, they cannot see that in their careless tramplings through this electronic proving ground, in an effort to flex and parade their intellectual capabilities, they are eroding the basic layers of security and trust which form the very foundation of any viable communications network. In the same way that emotional abuse is often more detrimental than its physical counterpart, this white-collar sport is no less criminal, and no less despicable, than the more common breaking and entering.

Revenge. The secretary who was refused a raise. The professional who was overlooked for a coveted management position. The last systems manager who was fired for not having done a backup in 3 years. This person's motive is revenge, and the amount of damage he or she can do will vary in direct proportion to the level of protection you have put in place less the level of technical ability and determination the avenger has.

Finally there is vandalism, which is really no motive at all. Vandals are merely thrill seeking, and they get their thrills by messing with your data. The damage they inflict ranges from the electronic mailbox basher equivalent (let's see if we can bring the network performance to its knees) to the arsonist or bomb tosser type (let's try to log on and reformat the server drive). Vandals are challenged by overcoming security measures and doing as much damage as possible. Protecting your systems against this type of low-life means adopting a paranoid's view of the world, because without more reasonable motives it is hard to predict a vandal's behavior. You just have to assume the worst.

Solutions

Knowing the various motives behind unauthorized data access helps to pinpoint what systems are at risk from what type of access. This will in turn point to some possible solutions.

Physical isolation is the most effective and dramatic approach to security. Though extreme, sometimes it is warranted. For top-secret data worth millions of dollars, it may be the only reasonable solution. Remove the floppy drives and eliminate the possibility of data being copied to diskettes. Remove any phone connections and eliminate the chance for a thief to come in through the communications window. Add additional layers of protection by having keycard access to the room housing the secure network, by installing password protection at various levels of access, and by changing the passwords constantly.

There are other security measures that are not as hard-core, but almost as effective, depending on the nature of the potential risk. You may have dial-in software to enable sales reps to call in from the road and access their prospect data. You could disable this capability, but at a high cost to productivity. Better to make sure that only authorized employees can access the system. There are two common ways to ensure this. One is with password protection, and the other is through dialback software. The latter is the more secure of the two methods. You should recommend that this setup be standard procedure and eliminate packages that do not offer this option. Preset the software with the home phone number or car phone of the sales rep. When the rep (or an unauthorized person) makes a call into the sales rep's PC, the communications software hangs up and redials that preset number to establish the connection. An added benefit is that the phone call will be initiated and therefore covered by the company, thus cutting down on the need for expense reimbursements for phone bills. Knowing the phone number and password of an authorized person won't help unless you can also access the phone. This system is not totally without potential for security breaches, but it will eliminate a large window of illegal opportunity.

Many employees don't think twice about copying corporate data to floppies in order to do some work at home, and organizations are loathe to restrict this practice for the sake of what is perceived to be a minor security risk. However, systems security should allow only data at the lowest security level to be copied for this purpose. And strict policy should govern the handling of files used on home computers.

Sensitive data can be desensitized before it is copied to an area for more public use. Personnel data, without the name or other identifying fields, can be passed along for statistical or budgetary purposes without the potential of a security breach.

Password protection is a commonly used tool, but has some drawbacks. Unless passwords are long enough, and changed frequently enough, they do not represent a serious barrier. Unfortunately, the longer and more frequently changed the passwords are, the more likely that the user will need to write them down—a practice that also seriously compromises the security of the system. If people need to write down a password, they need to be very selective about where the password is stored. A wallet or a locked filing drawer may or may not be adequate protection, depending on the nature of the risk.

In reality, password protection can be more of an illusion than a buffer. A surprising number of password files are stored as .DBFs or as ASCII text files, without any encryption or access restrictions. While this may eliminate the casual breach, a dedicated snoop with any level of sophistication won't be slowed down at all. Another commonly overlooked security problem exists when managers do not disable the default passwords that come with password-protected software. Any half-witted hacker knows to try the default supervisor log-in in order to break into a network system, because surprisingly often this hole is left open.

There are times when even the most secure data have to leave the premises. Off-site backups are one case in point. If the value of information stored on your system is in the millions of dollars, surely off-site backups are mandatory, but how do you make sure they are protected? Some information should be encrypted before it leaves the premises so that it can reach its destination without being stolen by observant eyes. Electronic mail messages are usually encrypted while they wait in the public mailbox for transmittal to the recipient. This is an extra layer of protection that should be investigated for the higher security levels of data. If highly confidential data need to be sent through the mail or via common carrier phone lines, then encryption before sending may be warranted.

Systems Security Analysis

To conduct an unauthorized-access audit, you need to begin with the list of information systems you have compiled during your inventory

---

Systems Security Analysis

System: *Payroll*

Access should be limited to: *Payroll manager*

Access is limited by: *Network security*

Describe the physical connections to other computers in the organization: *On the network*

Describe the phone connections to this system directly: *None*

Describe the phone connections to networked systems: *Modem server*

What motives would interest internal parties in accessing this system, and what would be the consequence? *Curiosity—coworker wants to see. Likely—possibly damaging to morale. Revenge—ex-employee wants to mess things up. Unlikely—no serious consequences. Medium-level risk, worth taking protective measures.*

What motives would interest outside parties in accessing this system, and what would be the consequence? *Greed—competitor wants to see what we pay our people, and to get names for recruiting. Not likely, but it could be damaging. Low risk, not worth overprotection.*

Is the system safe from curious/ignorant access? *Yes—network security will prevent anyone without rights to access or even see this directory.*

Is the password file protected? *No*

Is the system safe from motivated, technically adept trespassers? *No. Anyone with supervisor rights can access payroll directory.*

Security rating: *Confidential*

Recommendation: *Enable the payroll password, and change twice per year. This will dissuade all but the most adept and determined hacker.*

> **Systems Security Analysis**
>
> System: *R&D*
>
> Access should be limited to: *R&D engineers*
>
> Access is limited by: *Network security and password control*
>
> Describe the physical connections to other computers in the organization: *On the network*
>
> Describe the phone connections to this system directly: *None*
>
> Describe the phone connections to networked systems: *Modem server*
>
> What motives would interest internal parties in accessing this system, and what would be the consequence? *Curiosity—employees wanting to know what we're working on. Challenge—see if they can break in. Greed—sell information to competition. Revenge—give competition our secrets out of spite. Consequences could be extremely serious if the information fell into the wrong hands. Minimize risk at all costs.*
>
> What motives would interest outside parties in accessing this system, and what would be the consequence? *Competitive greed. Extremely serious consequences. Potential value of the information makes the risk high.*
>
> Is the system safe from ignorant access? *Yes—network security will prevent anyone without rights to access or even see this directory.*
>
> Is the password file protected? *Yes—encrypted and stored in a restricted directory.*
>
> Is the system safe from motivated, technically adept trespassers? *No. Anyone with supervisor rights can access the R&D directories.*
>
> Security rating: *Top secret*

and criticality analysis. The Security Committee has assigned sensitivity ratings to the various applications, and now will examine not only the likely sources of a security breach but the implications and likelihood of the risk.

The actual audit is merely an assessment of the protective measures that are being taken vis à vis the security rating attached to any particular system. Unfortunately, with every additional protective measure, you will need to sacrifice something else, like efficiency or ease of use. Otherwise, why not protect everything from all possible risks? Every organization, every situation will differ with respect to the appropriate balance here. Your job is to make sure that the balance is consciously and conscientiously struck.

For each system, picture how each motive might play out. Examine each system identified during your criticality analysis, and determine where the threats to various systems come from, and how serious a violation would be. As many people as possible can participate in this discussion, since it's really a brainstorming session to help uncover the potential risks. Play the devil's advocate. Get paranoid. Why would unauthorized users want the information? What would they do with it? How could they get it? What would it mean? Finally, what should be done about it?

Examine the accompanying systems security analyses (pages 113 and 114). In each case, you need to identify both the likelihood and the implications of a security breach. By completing an analysis for each system, you will be forced to think about the implications of the various threats, and therefore to recommend the appropriate level of protection against unauthorized access.

Standard Security Precautions

Your security rating should reflect what protective measures should be taken. "Top secret" data, for instance, might require isolated systems and encrypted files. This category would be reserved for information which has a high monetary value to outsiders, and for which the implications of a security breach would be very serious.

"Secret" data might require quasi-isolated systems and frequent password changes. This label might be used to denote systems which would not be of tremendous value to competitors, but which should not be made public either. A database of AIDS patients might fall into this category.

"Confidential" data can reside on a public network with password protection and network security. This label might be suitable for most payroll systems. "Private" data require normal levels of protection against the ignorant or casual breach. "Public" data are just that.

Your situation may call for a different type of rating scheme altogether. The key is to group various systems logically, according to their security needs, and to apply security standards consistently.

Once you establish the level of security needed for each security rating, you need to determine the specific steps that will be taken, as illustrated in the chart on the next page. The actual protective measures

Security Rating	Protective Measures to Be Implemented
Public	No protection Access from menus All users have read/write authorization
Private	Limited protection Network security
Confidential	Network security Password protection Modem setup with dialback
Secret	Physically isolated network Log-in and system passwords No modem connections Forced password changes monthly Encrypted files Network security software
Top secret	Physically isolated network Log-in and system passwords No modem connections

you take will vary depending on the risks you face and the tools at your disposal.

To Do

- Assess the motives behind unauthorized data access.
- Identify the likelihood and implications of a security breach.
- Assign a security rating to each system.
- Establish protective measures.

Chapter 11

Preventive Maintenance

Purpose

Computers, like people, rarely die of old age. There are identifiable causes, and while eventual decay can't be avoided over the long haul, it can be postponed with the proper care and maintenance. By establishing preventive maintenance (PM) procedures and schedules, you will add years to the life of your organization's computers, and reduce the number of untimely failures.

You conducted your first PM during the initial walk-through inventory. At that time, depending on the conditions you found, you scheduled the date for the next PM. Now you can take the time to do a more thorough PM, expanding on the original preventive maintenance service report to include additional tasks (see pages 118–119).

Internal Tasks

To perform a PM you'll need to open up the machine, so it's best to ensure that a backup was done just prior to the PM. When you call to schedule the PM with the primary user, ask him or her to make sure that a full backup has been done. When you arrive for the PM, ask to make a copy of the backup log. This will verify that the backup has been done and will provide a backup audit at the same time.

Before you get started, take a look around and note any new environmental issues that may negatively affect the computer. Smoke, dust,

Preventive Maintenance Service Report	
Date:	CPU Number:
Technician:	Reason: (routine/request)
Primary user:	Phone:

Backups completed prior to PM: (attach copy of log)

Environment notes:

Internal status:

Vacuumed:

Reseat cards:

Check cables:

Check battery:

Replace battery:

Clean floppy drives:

Run hard-drive diagnostics: (attach results)

Run floppy-drive diagnostics: (attach results)

Surge suppression indicator check UL pass-through:

UPS check:

Rated life: _____

Capacity: _____

Test run life: _____

Total VA rating of supported equipment: _____ (attach worksheet)

Comments:

External cable check:

Keyboard shakeout:

Preventive Maintenance Service Report (Cont.)	
Boot disk files match:	
Boot disk directory attached:	
Other tasks:	Results/comments:
User comments:	
Other notes:	
Next service scheduled:	
Completion date:	Signature:

grease, heat, and large equipment operating nearby are some of the obvious things to look for.

When you open the machine, take notes on the status of the interior in order to help determine when to perform the next PM. If the inside is filthy, schedule your next PM for 3 months hence. If it's very clean, an annual PM is sufficient.

Vacuuming the inside of the computers will reduce the built-up heat caused by trapped dust. Video screens attract dust, and the pull of your power supply fan sucks it into your CPU, where it settles on your boards and circuitry. Under this dusty blanket, damaging heat builds up. Use a miniature vacuum to suck up all the loose dust in and around cards, the motherboard, the power supply, and the fan. Avoid touching anything with the nozzle. In tight spots it may be better to use a compressed-air spray can to blow the dust out.

Reseat cards and cables after vacuuming and after grounding yourself. Cable and board connections continually expand and contract as they undergo rapid temperature fluctuations. As a result, any nonsoldered parts can creep out of their connecting sockets, causing intermittent problems until they fully disconnect.

Replace batteries. Rather than waiting until batteries die and lose setup, take preemptive action and replace any batteries that are approaching their life expectancy. This will mean tracking the replacement date in a log or on the battery itself.

Once this task is complete, you can close the patient back up and go on to floppy and hard-drive maintenance.

Disk Hardware Maintenance

Clean the floppy-drive heads. Filthy heads increase the chances of data-read errors, and the dirt can be transferred to floppy disks and damage whatever data is stored on them. Head-cleaning kits are available through any office supply catalog.

Run the disk diagnostics to show any indications of problems on both the hard drives and the floppy drives. (These tests will also be run during your hard-drive maintenance audit, which you can schedule 6 months after your PM for maximum coverage.) Running disk diagnostics every 6 months is appropriate even for a healthy disk. If tests show signs of problems, more frequent checkups may be called for.

Power PM

The next aspect of your PM tests your system's ability to process and protect itself from the power it receives. Too much power can obviously harm a computer system. Even though spikes are short, they can carry a tremendous overload of power. Surges tend to be less dramatic in terms of the voltage they deliver, but since they last longer, they too can damage hardware over time. While a spike is not a common occurrence, it is greatly feared because of the immediate and catastrophic results. Lightning is the most common cause of a spike, and the delivery of such huge amounts of power can ruin a piece of equipment, corrupt data, or cause momentary malfunction of equipment.

While lightning comes most quickly to mind when one thinks about too much power, a more likely culprit will be switching large electrical loads on or off, either within the facility or on the power line during utility switches.

Noise and other distortions are significant not in the volume of power they provide but in their extraneous and potentially confusing nature. Radio frequency (RF) transmissions, perhaps the most common form of noise, can occur when computer equipment has not been properly protected to reduce radio emissions. RF interference can cause data errors and strange behavior, but does not damage components. Distortions that arise from intermittent power use (fax machines, copiers, fans, etc.) have the potential to cause not only errors but damage.

Too little power can come in the form of sags, brownouts, or blackouts. Sags are the opposite of surges, and result when too little power is provided from undersized power systems, or when a large electrical load is introduced onto your power line. Terminals, especially VGA monitors, are more sensitive to low power conditions and may shut off. More seriously, disk-read errors or head crashes can also result from power sags.

If sags last minutes or more, they are more accurately tagged as brownouts. If the power is discontinued altogether, then the condition is described as blackout. Sudden loss of power can damage equipment, and the interruption midprocess of systems events has some obvious and serious ramifications.

The power supply in each PC carries a minimum level of protection, up to perhaps 800 V. This means that if a surge of 800 V comes through the line, your built-in power supply will pass through only 120 V. While this level of protection will cover the majority of daily surges, it is not uncommon to experience surges between 800 V and 6000 V. To hedge your bets against the more powerful surges, as well as against damage that can occur from low power, you'll want to look at further protection.

There are three general categories of protective equipment to help with power problems. The most common (and least expensive) protective devices are *surge suppressors*. Their purpose is to filter out spikes, surges, and RF interference. This minimal level of protection should be used to protect all equipment, including phone lines. It's not uncommon for the computer power line to be protected, but to have damage occur through the modem phone line.

The surge suppressor market is flooded with products, and it's difficult to make an intelligent choice among the myriad of products, which range in price from $19.95 to several hundred dollars. How do you choose? You want the system to protect against voltage levels above 500 V so that your power supply has a margin of protection. Buy only products tested by Underwriters Laboratories (UL), and look to see that the UL pass-through voltage is less than 500 V. You should also use products that indicate the level of suppressor activity. Most products' ability to protect degrades over time. The products then begin reacting to less and less significant surges, or they may fail altogether, allowing damaging spikes to pass through. Buy surge protectors with indicators which will reveal when surge protection is no longer active. These criteria will eliminate many cheaper brands, but not all, and price alone is not a valid indicator of a product's effectiveness. The existence of surge suppression on all lines connected to the PC should be checked, as should their protection status. Check also that surge protectors are never strung together, since this will create an unnecessary fire risk.

The next level of protection is found in *line conditioners.* These offer longer-term handling of power discrepancies during sags and brownouts and handle more distortion conditions. These units may cost several hundred dollars, and are not warranted to protect inexpensive equipment with low-level data. When you need to prevent a total loss of power from wreaking havoc on a network or some other critical operation, then you will need to have UPS protection. The primary purpose of the UPS is to allow for graceful degradation, not battery backup for ongoing use. Most UPS systems are designed to give you less than an hour, and more typically only 10 to 20 minutes—just long enough to get everyone off the system and shut off any outstanding processes. The price for a UPS will depend primarily on how much capacity you need.

If you need to ensure uptime for extended periods (hours, days, or weeks) regardless of power supply, then you will have to look at *uninterrruptible battery systems* (UBS). These will cost thousands of dollars, and should be reserved for only the most critical applications. Most are operated with gasoline or diesel fuel.

UPS VA Requirements				
Equipment	Volts	Amperes	Watts	VA
			Subtotal	
			Growth multiplier	
			Total VA required	

More sophisticated systems allow you to monitor your environment and UPS equipment on an ongoing basis, alerting you to dangerous or potentially dangerous conditions. At a minimum, you should check the status of your UPS by pulling the plug and timing its ability to retain power. This should naturally be done only after a full backup, and when no one is processing.

To determine whether the UPS is of adequate size, you need to establish the total volt-ampere (VA) rating of all the equipment connected to the UPS. On a UPS VA requirements form, list all the equipment that will be protected by the UPS. You will find either voltage and amperage listed, or wattage. If you find the voltage and amperage, simply multiply the two to get the VA rating, which goes in the last column. If you find the wattage, multiply the number by 1.43 to get the VA figure.

Add up the VA column and put this number in the subtotal column. Depending on the growth you expect to the system being supported by the UPS, enter a multiplier in the space provided. Use at least 10 percent to give yourself a cushion. When you add the growth factor to your subtotal, you will get the required VA. When selecting a UPS, make sure it is rated for at least this amount. Remember that each component plays a part. Your monitors, printers, and modems have a load associated with them, as does your computer.

External Once-Over

After completing the power tests, make a visual check of the cables for any loose connections, frayed shielding, or rat's nest tangles. Shake out the keyboard over a trash can to loosen up any paperclips or other debris that may short something later. Look for the boot disk and make sure it's up to date. Are the startup files up to date?

List any other tasks that you performed during your PM, along with comments or notes. Attach reports, directory listings, or any other data that may be helpful now or historically. Ask the primary user whether there have been any problems. While in theory these problems would be logged with the help desk, there may be intermittent problems that have never been reported.

The date of this machine's next PM will depend on its criticality rating, its age, the environment, and your findings during the current PM. If you schedule service sooner than 1 year, make note of why. Fill out a PM service report that shows the results of the services performed and identifies the schedule for the next PM. This information can also be entered into a database to indicate trends and patterns.

Whenever the top needs to be popped, consider using the opportunity to do a PM. With regular service, the machine will last longer and have fewer problems.

To Do

- Establish PM procedures and schedules.
- Schedule internal maintenance for all machines.
- Schedule disk hardware maintenance for all machines.
- Schedule power supply audits.

Chapter 12

Source Code Audits

Purpose

The MIS department is in full control of all the custom programs it has running on mainframes and minicomputers. A program isn't released for production until it has passed the alpha and beta testing phases and been documented and backed up for future revision management.

In your world, there may be no control over who's developing what. As a result, you don't even know what's out there, never mind whether it has been properly tested or documented. The situation opens the organization up to a lot of unnecessary risks. Losing carelessly backed-up custom software can represent the loss of hundreds, even thousands, of hours. A coding error can mean erroneous reports and cause grievous damage through misinformation and the actions taken because of it.

One of the goals of distributed processing is to get the tools into the hands of the end user so that he or she can develop the systems needed without turning to MIS. Still, you need to know what's out there, what it's being used for, and whether special measures must be taken in order to provide security for critical applications.

Where to Find Custom Applications

You will locate custom applications in your software inventory. The primary user of the application (who may or may not be the key programmer) provided a basic description of the application and helped you

Application Audit Form	
Date:	Auditor:
Application name:	Revision:
Description:	
Key programmer:	
Criticality rating:	Security rating:
Tools used:	
Were the appropriate sets of systems documentation found? Does it match with current structures and data? Do revision numbers match? Where are copies kept?	
User documentation notes: (attach) Source code samples: (attach) Source code documentation notes: (attach) Recommendations for performance improvements: (attach)	
Data input source: Output description/samples: (attach) Testing methods: (attach)	
Custom application library has latest backup of source: Check off-site backups of latest executable code Check off-site backups of latest application source code Check off-site backups for this version of documentation	
Are version control procedures being followed? Is version control log up to date?	
User comments:	
Follow-up notes and comments:	
Next audit date scheduled:	
Sign-off:	Date:

determine an appropriate criticality and security rating. Now it's time to return to ask a few more questions.

What does the application do? Who wrote it? Has it been tested? Where is the documentation kept? Where are backups to the source code kept? Finally, how are revisions managed? Use an application audit form (see page 126) to help gather this information.

Each custom application ought to have one person with the assigned responsibility for that application. That person will usually be the developer of the application or the project leader in the case of a group effort. Your job is to show these key people what needs to be done to properly manage an application, and to audit them from time to time in order to ensure that the policies for application management are being adhered to. Each key programmer will help you fill out the application audit form.

Security Ratings

The criticality rating should be based on how important a program is to the operation of the department or company. Critical operations need to be very closely managed because of their vital importance, but noncritical applications cannot be ignored. Many programs that begin as ancillary shortcuts become mission-critical operations as time goes on. Others may lessen in importance over time, and you'll need to uncover these changes and modify the level of control you install accordingly.

The key programmer may be found at the department level, but for critical applications a much closer connection to your department must be maintained. In particular, you need to be alerted to any changes being made to these critical programs. Establish a central location for the source code, and check out the source code when changes are needed to ensure your foreknowledge.

The security rating measures how controlled the access to this application and its data needs to be. A high security rating may have implications for how backups are done and where they are stored, as well as for additional tests that may be required to validate the security methods built into the software.

Development Tools and Documentation

What version of what products was used in the development of this application? Needless to say, you should have a valid license to use the development tools, and the tools themselves should be backed up and monitored.

Locate the information about the input source, file structures, variables, and other systems parameters that any person working with the application will need to know. Is it complete? Up to date? Create a list of the file structures, the data elements, and the indexes being used. If the application was written with a tool that has built-in systems documentation capabilities, this effort will be easier. (You may want to consider banning tools that do not offer this facility.) These documents can be used for comparison against the stored systems documentation to make sure that the latest revisions are being recorded. If revision numbers are used, check for cross-references between the systems documentation and the application. Two copies of this documentation should be available: one off-site and the other in the applications library.

Whether the document is a one-page sheet of instructions or a 400-page bound manual, the user of an application should have some guideline to follow. A minimum of three sets of this documentation should be kept: one off-site, one in the applications library, and one with the key user.

Take a look at the code, or samples of code, to see how well it has been documented. Will it be easy for someone other than the responsible person to make changes? Does the structure of the code facilitate debugging and modifications? Are there obvious improvements that could be made?

Input/Output and Testing Methods

Find out the source of the data used for input to this application. Get descriptions and samples of the output.

Find out what tests were used to validate the code. The more critical the application, the more important the testing. Are there parallel manual systems that can be used to benchmark the application? Can the results be verified as obviously wrong or right through a simple visual check? Have tests been run to show how the application deals with the extreme or unusual cases? A well-presented printed report can be dangerously authoritative, leading users to jump to the conclusion that the results are beyond reproach. Put together checks that can be used and apply them.

Backup Security

Where are off-site backups of custom applications? A copy of the latest source code, executable code, and documentation of any custom software should be kept off-site. In addition, the custom application library should house all the sources for every revision of every custom application. Library records will facilitate backtracking and troubleshooting should the need arise. Backups of the source code should be done separately and in addition to any source code that is backed up normally during daily and other regular backup processes. Regular backups alone are not adequate since they will be recycled over time. An isolated backup of the source code, stored with the revision information, keeps each version separately and permanently.

These copies of the source code should be made as closely to the last compilation time as possible. Backups taken weeks or months later may contain corruptions that will not be apparent until a recompile is done.

Revision Management

Revision management will keep the application development process going smoothly. Each time a change is contemplated for an operational system, a revision request should be completed and approved before

Application Revision Request	
Date:	Filed by:
Application name:	
Application location:	
Reason for revision:	
Details:	
Revision request authorization:	Date:
Revision completed by:	Date:
Documentation revised by:	Date:
Revised system backup:	Date:
Sign-off:	Date:

the change is made. This procedure will ensure that modifications aren't made too hastily, and that any changes are duly recorded and backed up.

A large application may have a revision manual that tracks the many changes made over the years. A formal revision numbering scheme should be implemented and rigidly controlled. A smaller application may have a file folder with notes and one-page user and system documentation included. In both cases, however, it is important to establish a system that logs all revisions.

User comments

Ask the primary user of the application for feedback. You may find out that the program is slow, lacks certain features, or is otherwise in need of modification.

Follow-up

The result of your audit should be a list of action items that need to be taken. The more critical the application, the more critical the action items. Any of the inadequacies you have uncovered need to be corrected. Identify who will do what and by when. Include a follow-up date to review the action items, and once everything has been addressed, set a date for the next audit. All programs should be reviewed at regular intervals while they are in use, and the higher an application's criticality and security rating, the shorter the interval between audits. Revisions made to a program may trigger the need for an audit sooner than would otherwise be the case, as will the findings of any particular audit.

Modified Commercial Software

There are truthfully only two kinds of software: commercial and custom. Many commercial products are modifiable, either in the sense that file structures and field names can be modified or in the sense that the actual source code can be changed. In the latter case, the entire program needs to be treated like a custom-developed program. Once you have modified the source code of a commercially available product, you're on your own. It should be considered as an inexpensive shortcut to the completely custom solution, and therefore a happy compromise. However, keep in mind that with the first change, you've veered off the path of shrink-wrap. It is up to you to manage the software rather than the vendor.

It is important not only to keep track of the source code but to make a list of the changes and the reasons for them. When new releases of the commercial package are available, the decision will have to be made as to whether to upgrade. Usually, upgrading means having to reincorporate the changes you've made into the new product, so you need to know what changes will be necessary. In many cases, changes made to the original product will be incorporated into later releases of the commercial package and will hence be unnecessary as custom work.

Should you upgrade once customizations have been made? This decision needs to be carefully considered because of the added expense. Also, not upgrading will mean that you've divorced yourself further from the commercial product. As future upgrades pass you by, you will be less able to get support from the vendor, and important enhancements will not be available.

To Do

- Review software inventory for a list of custom applications.
- Establish central custom applications library.
- Determine off-site location for backups.
- Schedule initial round of audits.

Part 4

Support Issues

Chapter 13

Help Desk

Objectives

The help desk is really just a formalization of the helping functions that you have been providing all along. You, your company, and your fellow employees all stand to gain from the benefits that a good help desk can provide. Staff members will get quicker response and resolution to their problems, you will be absolved of having to solve the same problem over and over, and the company will see less time wasted on troubleshooting and resolution of problems.

On the other hand, if it is poorly set up or administered, the help desk can add to the problems and frustrations that people experience, increasing costs to the company. How do you ensure that you create a help desk that contributes to rather than hinders the achievement of these objectives?

The first component of a successful help desk is a clearly defined mission. The impetus for starting up the help desk is usually a growing number of frustrated users who are in turn frustrating the existing support staff. So the obvious mission of the newly formed help desk is to provide an organized approach to solving user computer problems. But you'll have to give some thought as to which users are being supported—what level of problems, through which technologies, in what capacity, and at what stage of the support process.

Without a clear objective, your help desk staff may set goals that are counterproductive to your purpose. You may think it's obvious that your role is to resolve problems, but your staff may see resolution as simply pointing to the solution. A employee calls to say that her spreadsheet won't load. Is resolution of the problem defined by identifying that she needs more memory, or by installing the memory and having her successfully load the spreadsheet? Is the help desk responsible for suggesting training for employees who repeatedly call with certain basic questions?

Some help desks are broken down by functional division, with one group supporting engineers, another group supporting the sales and administrative functions, and yet another help desk dedicated to operations. This arrangement is common when the hardware, software, and typical user questions vary widely among different functional groups. Other help desks are defined up by the nature of the problem. Users are directed to call one area for hardware, and another for software. The problem is that users frequently don't know whether a given problem is related to hardware or software, and often it's a combination of the two. A third division of labor is to set up help desks according to the severity of the problem. All calls are routed to the primary help desk initially, and they may be elevated to another help desk depending on the nature of the problem.

Several other key issues must be decided. Will the help desk staff fix hardware or call in support for this function? Will users go to the help desk for help, or will the help desk provide support at the user's workstation? Is the help desk a phone support function or does it have training facilities and technical workshop areas? Will your help desk have any responsibility for analyzing the problems that it handles in order to provide proactive support to solve problems that it sees recurring, or will this function be carried out by another group?

An appropriate objective statement might be:

> The XYZ help desk has been organized to meet the needs of computer users throughout the organization for timely response and resolution to computer-related problems. Toward this end, the help desk will be the one call that an employee needs to make. Upon receiving a request for assistance, the help desk will organize the necessary resources to resolve the problem, and will provide the necessary follow-up to ensure that the problem is resolved to the satisfaction of the caller. Further, the help desk will be responsible for disseminating information that will help forestall problems, which become obvious from previous requests for help.

This statement of objective is loosely worded to allow flexibility in the methods and procedures used to resolve problems. However, two important features are clear: The help desk is ultimately responsible for problem resolution *and* for involvement in problem prevention. The mission statement should be followed by a description of the division of labor, scope of services, and other logistics that will help fulfill the mission.

Without the statement, you have no way of measuring your success and determining if you need to reevaluate your methods, or possibly your mission. Once you've done so, you need to let everyone know what your mission is. If you are the one call anyone experiencing a computer problem needs to make, you'll want to get the word out. When you staff your help desk, indoctrinate new members to your mission so that they understand their own role. One of the most debilitating aspects of help desk service is the it-ain't-my-job approach. This response will come about if people on the outside and on the inside of the help desk are unaware of its responsibilities.

Once you have determined why you're in existence, the best physical setup of your help desk will be more apparent: Form follows function. If you are providing phone support alone, you can be at any remote location. If you plan to do a lot of outreach, you'll need to be central to your clientele. Also, if users will be coming to you (for training, demonstrations, etc.), you'll need to have more accommodating facilities than would otherwise be necessary.

Skills and Attitudes

There are different philosophies with respect to user support and its role within the organization. While often unwritten and unspoken, the help desk philosophy will be obvious throughout the support staff. In order to make sure the philosophy is one you feel most benefits the organization, define and declare it up front. One very appropriate guiding principle is that of total quality. This means that it's always our job, the buck stops here, get the task done. This outlook is simple and fosters a can-do, helpful attitude.

The can-do approach

Another valid philosophy is that callers should be taught to solve the problem themselves whenever possible. This makes sense in that empowerment is a part of your job. Inspiring callers with a can-do attitude is a valid goal, but it can get turned around when the help desk is able to push the problem back on the caller. In many situations, it isn't appropriate for the caller to solve his or her own problem. Lacking the time, skills, and overall understanding of the technical strategy of your company, the user may not make the best choice among alternative solutions. If the help desk is left out of the loop, the best solution may go undiscovered and unimplemented. The primary danger with this philosophy is that it can set off a slow shift in attitude—from you-can-do-it to fix-it-yourself-it's-not-my-problem. While it makes sense to point out where in the manual a user can find an answer, a counterproductive RTFM (read the funny manual) mentality can seep in over time.

Equally bad is the little-red-hen-who-couldn't-get-anyone-to-do-it-so-she-did-it-herself philosophy. If the help desk makes dependent wimps out of callers, everyone suffers as a whole. The happy balance is one which gives callers not only the solutions to problems in a crisis but the tools to solve more and more problems on their own. There are often things that help desk technicians can do in solving a problem that help the caller understand what went wrong, and how to better troubleshoot problems in the future.

Once you've described your support philosophy, you'll have a better idea of what type of person you're looking for to staff your help desk. Attitude is by far the most important aspect of call handling. Help desk staff need to be patient, yet not patronizing. They must be good listeners, supportive, helpful, and conscientious about following through. Choose your phone staff carefully, and as soon as you suspect a mismatch, get that person off the front lines of the help desk. With the right attitude, your callers will forgive a lot, including lack of knowledge. However, if a help desk member takes a patronizing or arrogant posture, callers are going to be turned off, no matter how technically adroit the technician is. A problem staffer may simply have a misconception of what the help desk's role and responsibilities are. Make sure that the mission, philosophy, and resulting roles are clearly spelled out.

Reinforce the importance of caller satisfaction by including caller feedback as a measure of job performance. The call support form at the end of this chapter includes initialization and comments from the caller as part of the sign-off process. It may not be feasible to solicit feedback for each problem, but regular feedback will provide the information you and your staff need to ensure that your mission is being carried out and that your philosophy is filtering through. If a clearly defined role and customer feedback don't result in the right attitude, there is simply a mismatch. Some personality types don't belong behind a help desk, and short of intensive psychotherapy you're probably not going to effect a change.

Listening skills

No one is born with innate listening skills. Everyone must learn them somewhere along the way. For the lucky ones who learned young, poor listening habits can seem like an unalterable character flaw in those who haven't learned yet. Fortunately, with the right attitude, the desire to learn, and some basic training, most of us can learn to listen better. There are many courses to help people develop active listening skills, but the bottom line is usually that the poor listener is simply too good at talking. Since you can't listen while you are talking, a very easy way to become a better listener is to try to talk less. Effective listening to computer problems is no different from effective listening in any other field. Many computer problems vanish in the telling, without the technician offering anything other than a responsive ear.

Asking the right questions is a skill, but just keeping the questions coming—which keeps the caller talking and the technician listening—is useful. It's not until all the facts have been collected (and the anger and frustration are out of the way) that the helper should offer a solution. By jumping in too soon, a help desk staffer may miss a critical fact and give an answer that doesn't solve the whole problem. Also, if the staffer tries to solve only the technical problem, ignoring the frustration, only half the caller's needs will be satisfied. A little sympathy along with the answer can make the difference between mere satisfaction and grateful appreciation.

Although listening is far and away the most important communications skill, the ability to speak and write cohesively is also important. One of the toughest things for technically trained people is to keep their language jargon free when talking to nontechnical people. We all use jargon, and some of yesterday's computer jargon is public domain today: PC, hard disk, RAM. It's simply a matter of use. Unfortunately, as we become accustomed to new technical terms, frequently we forget that they're still foreign to others. While it's acceptable and fun to talk techie among our peers, talking the same way to nontechnicians will cause anxiety, frustration, and even anger.

Here's a workshop idea that will help break your staff (and yourself) of "jargoneering," and at the same time provide nontechies with some answers to their technical questions. Get your techies together with an equal number or more of nontechies. Seat the technical folks across from and facing the nontechnical volunteers. Provide the nontechnical people with common questions that technical people will face in the field, or ask them to bring their own. The workshop involves having the nontechnical team ask a question of any tech team member, who must answer in plain English. The nontech team members raise their hands (or better a red flag) every time the tech team brings up a phrase they don't understand. The moderator keeps score, and takes down the techie phrases which raise the flag. The tech team gets a point if the question is answered without a flag being raised. The nontech team gets a point if the tech team uses jargon. This game can be played with teams from different departments asking questions of the technical team. (And why not have the technical team ask questions back?) At the end of the session, the team with the most points wins. The end result is a list of key phrases that the tech team has learned to rephrase, and a better understanding of the problems that nontechnical people have in dealing with technicians.

Follow-through

Follow-through is a valuable attribute that is three parts skill. Broken promises are usually the result of a well-intentioned technician who simply got busy and forgot. Technicians need to be trained to make only promises that are keepable, to write every promise down so it's not forgotten, and to assign reasonable follow-up dates so the task doesn't get continually put off.

What kinds of technical skills are important for the front-line staff? It's fairly obvious that staffing the help desk with highly experienced technical people is a waste of resources. Someone with less experience but with a technical background makes the best call manager. This staffer should have excellent listening skills and a broad knowledge of the hardware and software being used, so he or she can troubleshoot the basic problems and ask the right questions. These skills will solve 80 to 90 percent of the problems that get called in. For the remaining problems, the generalist can draw on the expertise of the old hands.

A nontechnical person will get thrown off course by every red herring, and route the caller to several experts who each in turn need the caller to reiterate the problem. The technogeneralist is more likely to know what questions to ask, and which expert to draw on, and will be able to provide just the information the expert needs, saving the expert and the caller valuable time.

Some standard questions are likely to be raised initially in order to help route the question and gather statistics. It may be tempting to give this task to a nontechie. Again, however, the technogeneralist will be able to bypass many of these preliminary questions without asking them, relying solely on the information the caller has given during the initial description of the problem. This avoids the frustration users experience when they have to answer seemingly obvious questions over and over.

Call Management

There are many software tools for call management and problem tracking. If the size of your help desk warrants it, you'll want to investigate and evaluate the alternatives. They will help you avoid losing track of requests for help, and will provide useful statistical information about the numbers and types of calls being handled. Whether automated or manual, your call management system will need to track a problem through to resolution. As the number of calls increases, prioritization and routing become management issues as well.

Logging the call is an essential first step if there is going to be any kind of follow-up and future analysis of calls. The more information tracked, the better. Unfortunately, there is an inverse relationship between the severity of a problem and a caller's patience with administrative details—which is how the caller views logging information. Callers take unkindly to being passed around from person to person in an effort to get a problem resolved. There are three basic ways to handle the initial call.

First, set up an administrative screen. Have a technical generalist initially log the question and take down information—the time and date of the call, the caller (name, ID, department), the type of request being made (hardware, software), the priority to be assigned (critical, ASAP, at your convenience), and perhaps a brief description of the problem. Cost effectiveness is the driving force behind this approach. Rather than tying up technically skilled people at this task, you rely on less expensive administrative workers. The problem is that the caller realizes that the administrative screen is not getting the problem resolved. It can be very frustrating for a caller to go through the red tape while his or her presentation material for a scheduled meeting has just disappeared. So if a screening process is to be used, keep the questions to a minimum—at least until after the problem has been solved. Once the panic is over, most people will be happy to fill in the blanks.

Second, have the technical generalists responsible for collecting the administrative data follow through to problem resolution. In this way, when someone places a help desk call, he or she reaches a technically competent person who manages the problem by calling in the necessary resources to bear. This solution eliminates buck passing and losing the problem under the rug or between the cracks. Often, through no poor intentions on anyone's part, a call that continues to get forwarded to increasingly more appropriate people never really gets there, and the caller is left wondering what's going on. When the person who initially picks up the phone is tagged with the responsibility for the call, this phenomenon disappears.

Finally, assign responsibility for people, departments, and divisions among the staff so that every employee knows who his or her help desk consultant is and will request that person specifically when a problem arises. This, in an ideal world, may provide the most personalized level of service to individual employees, who then feel that there is one person out there who is highly aware of what's going on with their own problems. The issue then becomes what to do when the primary contact

Support Issues

Call Support Form			
Open date:	Time:	Assigned:	Help number:
Caller number:	Name:		Phone:
Priority:	Due date:		
Description of problem: (See additional report)			
Resolution: (See additional report)			
Implications: (See additional report)			
Close date:		Caller initials:	
Caller comments:			
Identifiers:			Entered:
CC:			Copied:
Disposition of original:			Filed:
Sign-offs required:			Date:

is not available, and when one consultant is overburdened during certain times while another consultant is not being fully utilized.

Every call should be prioritized in the event that triage is necessary. Establishing the priority of the call is not always straightforward, and the priority of any request can change over time. Still, time management will be enhanced when a priority system is determined up front, with a due date attached to any request that is time-sensitive. Use the call support form on page 142 to build your own custom-designed document. The trick is to strike a balance between simplicity and depth. You want to collect as much information in as simple a format as possible.

Going Beyond the Call

Knowing when the problem is solved is not always straightforward. Certainly, solving the problem means resolving the issue posed by the caller. Consider again the spreadsheet user who isn't able to load her spreadsheet. Until she can load the spreadsheet, her problem has not been resolved. Simply identifying the problem as not having enough memory is a step in the solution, but should not be considered as the solution itself. The caller will have a definite feeling of problem resolution at a certain point (when she's able to load the spreadsheet), but deeper implications of the problem remain which may suggest a longer-term solution. Will increasing numbers of memory problems arise with the switch to a new version of the corporate spreadsheet package? Is adding more memory really the answer, or do you need to take a look at the spreadsheet application with an eye toward making it more memory-responsible? While the caller's satisfaction may point to one level of resolution, and a very important one, you need to go beyond that to look at the long-term implications of the problem. Your form should include an area designed to identify and answer these longer-term issues.

Much can be gleaned from reviews of the statistics gathered over the course of time. Look at the frequency of callers. What's the average number of calls per employee? Take the top 80 to 90 percent of callers and study them to see what can be done to help. Are these people calling because they don't have the confidence, skills, or temperament to solve the problems on their own? Could a training program or some other mechanism alleviate frustration?

Look at the frequency of problems in terms of software products. Are certain products causing the majority of the headaches? If so, what can be done to minimize them? Consider formal training, short seminars, expert development, handouts—whatever will work.

What are the hardware issues? What long-term implications do they speak to? Look at the comments made by callers. Technicians need immediate feedback on the comments. At the same time, you need to take a broad-based view of the comments made about each technician from a variety of callers. Score technicians and let them know how they rate. The best performers need to be recognized. The low performers need to know they can do better. By looking at the problems that have occurred in the past, you can prevent problems in the future.

To Do

- Write up a mission statement for the help desk.
- Write up the responsibilities for help desk staff.
- Put together an appropriate phone support log and form.
- Evaluate phone support software products.
- Put together an explanation of the new service to users.
- Schedule an audit to review caller comments on help.
- Schedule an audit to plan training and other preventive measures suggested by caller questions.
- Schedule a workshop with technical staff and department volunteers.

Chapter 14

Training

Training Philosophies

==Training is the link between technology and productivity.== Whether through osmosis, or formal classroom training, people need to absorb the necessary skills to make technology effective. A coherent training philosophy will engender a comprehensive training plan, which will in turn result in more fully utilized technology. Without a plan, learning happens haphazardly, and productivity gains are less striking.

It begins with a philosophy. Where does your organization stand on the issue of technology training? Are there any written statements to guide you? If anything has been written, it's a strong indication that training is taken seriously. In some companies, among certain professionals, continuing education is required. Other companies just feel strongly that training is important. These companies will often already have a training plan, a training department, a large training budget, and scheduled time allocated for each employee's ongoing training. If you work for one of these organizations, your role will be more as an adviser than an organizer. You will be able to point out the areas in which people need to be trained, and the training department will handle it from there.

You are equally likely however, to find yourself working for a company at the opposite end of the spectrum—one that disparages any formal training as a waste of both money and time. In this type of situation, your role is more important and at the same time more difficult.

Is training a right, a responsibility, or a privilege? Is it optional or mandatory? Does each employee determine his or her own training needs, or does the employee's supervisor choose? Is training required for all positions, at all levels, regardless of seniority, or are only certain personnel involved? Are promotions and/or pay tied to educational achievements? These are some of the philosophical questions that need to be addressed before you are ready to develop a training plan and budget.

Here are two very different, but equally clear and valid philosophical statements:

Technical Training Objective 1 At [your firm name here] we believe that technical training is a continuing process needed to keep our employees' skills up to date so that our company can maintain its competitive position in the industry. We feel that the responsibility for planning one's own continued education should rightfully fall to the employee, while we accept the responsibility of paying for this training, since it should be of direct benefit to the corporation. We feel so strongly about the importance of training that promotions, raises, and, indeed, continued employment will be based upon the employees' continued commitments to and achievements in this area.

Technical Training Objective 2 At [your firm name here] we believe that technical training is often required for an employee facing new technologies on the job. When the need for training is apparent, an employee or his or her supervisor can apply for time and budget resources. The company retains the right to reject any application which it feels is not in the best interest of the company or for which more informal, on-the-job type training will suffice.

These basic philosophies will play out very differently when it comes to setting expectations and goals, plans, and budgets. If your philosophy is closer to the second approach, not much planning will happen. Training issues will be handled on an ad hoc basis by an employee's supervisor. If your philosophy is closer to the first approach, you will want to establish a technology training subcommittee and examine how this objective will be carried out in terms of the type of training people will receive, when it will happen, how it will be recorded, and so on.

A subcommittee made up of people from all departments should begin by formalizing the company's position with respect to training, and then work to establish goals to help meet the training objectives of the company. The subcommittee will look at the training needs within the company, the training formats that will be used, who will be trained, and how.

Let's look at some of the issues the group will have to tackle.

Training Triggers

What events will trigger a training response? When should training be scheduled? There are three basic approaches to determining when training is needed, along with several hybrids of these three basic ideas. The right combination for your organization will depend on the philosophy you espouse and the environment you're in.

The most common approach is to wait for an employee to ask for training because he or she wants to learn, or for a supervisor to stumble upon a gap in an employee's knowledge and request training. This approach has many problems, the most important being that the employee will often be unaware of the weak areas in his or her knowledge base. There is the secretary who "knows WordPerfect" but has never taken any word-processing training and uses the computer much like a typewriter, hitting RETURN after every line. There is the shipping clerk who sums up a column of figures by calculator before entering the total on the electronic spreadsheet, not realizing that there's a SUM function to learn about. The employee doesn't know that he or she doesn't know. The supervisor, looking at the results, doesn't know there's a problem. People who should be trained are likely to be overlooked.

A second approach is to assume that whenever a person's job changes, or whenever a new technology is put in place, training should occur. Don't test; just assume that training is needed. A drawback here is that some people will be trained in areas in which they are already proficient. Another drawback is that, without testing, you simply assume that anyone who has taken the training now has the knowledge. Big assumption.

The last approach to determining the need for training is to test for it. When an employee comes on board (or before), you may want to test for basic computer literacy. There may be a minimum level of computer literacy that is expected among all personnel with microcomputer workstations on their desks. Further, there may be certain additional skills that are expected of people performing certain jobs, or performing at certain levels within a given job function. Annually, or upon changing jobs, people will be tested for certain skill levels.

You will have to develop these tests yourself to reflect your company's environment and needs. Make the tests telling enough to pinpoint specific areas in which training may be needed. Start with the skills list for a particular job. If it is a secretarial position, the list may include:

Typing skills

Spell checking

Columns

Forms

Character formatting

The goal of every test question should be to uncover the need to train in one particular area. How will you test spell-checking ability? What test will show an ability to format?

Overcoming Barriers to Learning

Testing should be administered in a nonthreatening way if possible, so that employees are not terrified of exposing their lack of knowledge. Explain that the tests are designed, not to provide a pass/fail score, but rather to highlight areas in which an employee needs training. If training is seen, not as a punishment or some necessary evil to be dispensed with, but as an ongoing process that continues throughout every employee's career, then there is less fear involved in embarking on the process.

Several large emotional barriers need to be broken down before people will accept training as something other than a burdensome task. One big block against training lies in the fear of looking stupid. In order to learn, people have to accept their role as the unlearned. Many employees who feel they've done their time in schools and universities see the idea of training as a regression, not progress. In today's world, every employee obviously needs to overcome this view.

Another problem is that people view training as an interruption to their more important daily routine. Current technology has enabled workers to do things 10 times faster than before, but now, rather than having 10 times more leisure time, people just expect more to be done. Unlike a computer, the human brain doesn't absorb things instantly. As a result, training seems like a huge burden in an already crowded day.

Then there's fear of change. Very few people relish the world shifting beneath their feet, and being faced with new technologies and new ways of doing things. A common and understandable reaction is to run for the shelter of the way things have always been done. In their heart of hearts, employees know this reluctance is counterproductive, but the attitude persists, and you'll have to deal with it.

Knowing why people don't jump forward and say "train me" will help you uncover ways to find out who needs training anyway. Learn which employees will benefit from training the most, and how to go about drawing them toward increased enlightenment without scaring them off. If everyone spends a certain amount of time being trained each year, then the stigma of being singled out as a dummy is removed. If even high-level executives and people with many years of seniority still get training, the message goes out that training is an ongoing process rather than something to outgrow.

Training Formats

Once you have ascertained, one way or another, who needs to be trained in what, you have to determine how best to accomplish the training. There are many ways to train people, including formal classroom sessions, independent study plans, and workshops and seminars. Each format has its pros and cons and will succeed to varying degrees with different people and in different circumstances. What may work for secretaries won't necessarily work for engineers. What will please engineers may not fly with the managerial staff. And don't even whisper the word "training" near an executive.

Formal classroom training is the traditional method of instruction and has its merits for teaching large numbers of people a certain baseline of knowledge. An introductory course in word processing for all new clerical staff is an example. In many cases, however, classroom training is an increasingly outmoded method for adults in the workforce. It is often inefficient and inappropriate. In order to minimize the cost of training per student, organizations group a large number of people together from widely divergent levels, stick them in a classroom away from their work environment, and teach them from an academic study plan. The problem is that some of the students get lost because the material is over their heads, some don't learn anything because it's a rehashing of stuff they already know, and some simply can't absorb 6 straight hours of input. Other students can't make the leap from academic theory to real-world problems. Still other don't learn because they're not feeling well, are too tired, or had a fight with their spouse the night before. It looks cost-effective on paper, but the actual cost may be surprising. People usually learn better on a one-on-one basis than they do in groups. People absorb new information more easily when it is served up in smaller chunks over time. People understand better when there is a direct link between what they are learning and what they'll be doing in the next week on the job.

Workshops attempt to address some of the problems of more formal classroom training. They are typically smaller and shorter, and focus on hands-on instruction. This approach is ideal for advanced training and for training groups of people who will be working together.

Demonstrations presume that all you need to do is show people once and they'll take away the knowledge they need. At introductory sessions, demonstrations can give people a better idea of what a new technology is all about than can written or verbal descriptions. They can help reduce the fear of the unknown and provide an overview, giving students the big picture before the details are presented. However, a demonstration is not usually sufficient on its own to complete the training process.

Roundtables, user groups, and panel discussions are all ways to bring peers together to share and learn from one another. The informality is both a strength and a weakness. Participants can pull the agenda one way or another, as in a call-in radio show, to reflect the interests of the group. On the other hand, because there is less control over the material that will be discussed, certain important areas may never get covered. In this case, you're better off with a more structured format. For you as the coordinator, a panel or roundtable format relieves you of the responsibility of having to know more than the participants—a task that will be difficult if you have professionals using a certain product all day long. The panel format takes advantage of their skills, giving the experts a chance to show off and their peers a great opportunity to pick up on what the experts know.

Independent study is another efficient format in terms of resources, since no teacher is needed. It requires a highly motivated student who can set goals and be self-disciplined enough to follow through. Most students have great difficulty being given a directive to learn something new, without any feedback or direction. Usually they'll open up the manual and drop face first into it within minutes. For the most motivated students, the format can work well.

Perhaps the best of all worlds is the coaching method. This is a combination approach that takes some of the better parts of each format. It offers the guidance and knowledge of the classroom teacher in the form of the coach. It provides the hands-on training of the workshop. It is one on one, and flexible enough to solve real problems while communicating new technology and techniques. Coaching is administered at the student's workstation. The new technology is introduced to solve a problem that the student is facing. Lessons are typically 2 hours or less so as not to overload the student, and the coach leaves the student with homework that will be reviewed during the next session. At the end of the coaching session, the student not only has learned something new but has created something useful. The lesson sticks because it has immediate and direct payoff.

Training the Trainers

Who will do the training? Formal training requires formal training, and you'll have to determine whether you have the in-house resources available or whether you need to outsource the training function. Even coaches and other in-house experts should have training in training to ensure that they are able to make the most of their expertise. On the other hand, professional trainers can lack the real-world experience that would make them most helpful.

If training is an important component of employee measurement, then you'll have to maintain a database of the training and skills that each employee acquires.

To Do

- Establish a technology training subcommittee.
- Develop a training philosophy.
- Develop a training plan.

Chapter 15

Special Skills Development

Executive Training

Executive training is a special category of training. Put your social worker cap on and think for a minute. Executives are highly professional, talented, educated people who have accumulated years of experience and seniority. They are probably of the old school, which holds that, after reaching a certain level, workers are actually done growing and can turn their experience to the good of the organization by helping others grow. While today's executives are smart enough to realize that no one can afford to stop growing, they still view training as an onerous chore at best. When approaching the subject of executive training, keep in mind the respect that is an executive's due and the threat that you may pose.

Mistake number one is to come into the executive's office prepared to impress. As you busily show the CFO all you know, you are also parading his or her ignorance. Don't be surprised, then, when you get bristles rather than whistles as you display your vast stores of knowledge. Keep in mind that this person also has expertise in some area, and in that area you are a floundering neophyte. In your talks, take some time to find out what that expertise is and then ask relevant questions. The executive will enjoy teaching you, and you'll learn a couple of things yourself. The dialogue will also create a more positive and balanced relationship between the two of you. While you're on the receiving end of the expertise, notice how you feel. Anything that rubs you the wrong way, or that makes you feel OK about learning, probably affects the other person in the same manner. That's not to say you should give tit for tat. The exec may preach to you, talk down to you, confuse you with jargon. Don't turn around and do the same. Recognize what it is that irritates you and make sure you avoid it in your behavior. You may set the example and have it returned.

Mistake number two is to assume you know what executives need to know. Remember that they have achieved a level of command, and now in this possibly threatening situation you are telling them how their training will proceed. Again, they bristle. Find out what their expectations are, what they want to learn. Mold your training to their needs.

Mistake number three is to be patronizing. Nobody likes being treated as passé, particularly a senior exec who sees you as the next generation ready to sweep him or her under the rug. You need to be the

---

Sample Memo on Executive Coaching

DATE: [Insert]

TO: Executive

FROM: Executive's boss

SUBJECT: Executive coaching

We are well aware of the need to embrace new technology to help us keep our competitive edge and maximize our productivity with the increasingly limited resources at our disposal.

At the executive level this need is paramount, for unless we can understand and incorporate these changes into our work, we will not make the right decisions for others or be able to expect others to do likewise.

While this means that we can no longer rest on our laurels and expect what we've learned along the way to carry us through, it does not have to be an unpleasant, demoralizing experience. In fact, we're hoping you'll enjoy the opportunity to learn something new.

To this end, we are providing executive coaching on a regular basis to ensure that you get the information and the technology you need, along with the personal assistance you need to feel comfortable using the tools we have today.

[Your name here] will be calling you in the next couple of days to schedule your first monthly technical assistance meeting. These will be private sessions, typically 30 minutes each, during which [Your name here] can show you how to use any software or hardware you wish to learn about, answer any questions, help you set up shortcuts in the way you're doing things, and more.

In your first meeting, it will important for you to explain what you're using your computer for today, and any specific things you would like to achieve in future meetings.

If you have any questions, please don't hesitate to call me.

coach, the partner, the right hand of the person you are about to assist. Trust and respect are key.

The memo on page 154 is designed to introduce the executive coaching sessions, explain their purpose, and get the ball rolling. If possible, the memo should come from the executive's boss so that it carries the right weight and protects you from looking impertinent.

Your first meeting is going to set the tone for future sessions, so bear in mind whom you're dealing with and find out as much as you can about this person and what he or she is trying to accomplish. Remember that executives are not inherently as interested as you are in technology, but they will become interested in it if you can show them how it will help them accomplish their goals.

You should know what kind of hardware they are using and what kind of software they have on their system. Don't expect executives to be able to tell you this type of technical stuff, and if you throw out these questions, they're likely to be interpreted as intimidating. Also, realize that some of the information on an executive's computer may be confidential. You can't just start bringing up files without permission.

Come prepared with questions, and come prepared to do a lot of listening. Your job during this meeting is to find out how you can help. The ease of your task will depend on how forthcoming the exec is. You may walk into the CFO's office and get five questions succinctly placed before you. The CEO down the hall, on the other hand, may have 50 burning questions but a very strong fear of letting you know how little he or she knows. You're going to have to build up trust. Get people talking. Ask questions and then shut up and listen. When the executive is through, go over your notes to make sure you understand, and come up with a plan of attack. Keep every meeting short and focused, and whenever possible leave the office on a high note, having shown the exec something of value or having solved a problem. Finally, never discuss with others any privileged information that may come into your possession through these sessions. Your reputation and your job are at stake.

Secretarial Training

More and more, secretaries will need to be facile with computer applications that can help them get organized and keep staff organized. Software that helps with mailing lists, record keeping, and scheduling should be a part of every good secretary's arsenal. Yet few have had formal training, and many don't know there's an easier way to do things than what they're doing now. Find out what secretaries are doing, and come up with a set of tools that will help them with these tasks. Provide group or one-on-one training as needed, and you'll soon add exponentially to their productivity.

Every secretary with a computer engages in word processing, and with each new product introduced into the word-processing market, the possibilities and potentials get broader. Yet most secretaries know only a small percentage of the functions their word processors are capable of. Formal training is appropriate for teaching the basics because at this level there is a common pool of skills that you want everyone to absorb. While the day-long format of today's formal training sessions is not conducive to learning 6 hours of material, the secretary will pick up on the requisite basics. Out of a full day in the class, only 2 or 3 hours of material will probably be absorbed. If you can set up formal on-site training, you can adapt these classroom sessions to a more realistic expectation for adult attention spans—perhaps 2 hours.

With more advanced skills, the full-day training session produces even less payback, since the specific skills are likely to be different for each person. Also, by their nature, classes are removed from the real-life scenarios which they must be transferred to. Something funny happens when people who learn and feel comfortable in a classroom take that knowledge back to a slightly different environment. At the first frustration, when things don't work exactly as they did in class, the student gives up and goes back to old habits.

One secretary may need to know how to do footnotes and create indexes, another to set up margins and to create a columnar format. In the more formal setting, both leave at the end of the day having learned many things they have no immediate use for. By the time the application does arise, they may have forgotten what they learned.

The Word-Processing Users Group

As an alternative to the formal training approach, try getting this group together regularly, maybe six times per year, for less formal group learning. Send out a memo to managers asking them for the names of the main word-processing users in the department, and permission for them to meet for an hour every other month to discuss word-processing tricks and techniques which will make them more productive and efficient.

When you get feedback from the departments, issue a separate memo (see page 158) to possible members, inviting them to the first meeting. That meeting should describe the goal of the group and the sessions: to foster in-house expertise and to share knowledge among users. Go around the group with introductions, and find out what kinds of things people are working on. There will be a lot of letters, various

Sample Memo to Department Managers

DATE: [Insert]

TO: Department head

FROM: Your name

SUBJECT: Word-processing users group

We are forming a word-processing users group for those people in the organization who spend a good deal of their time working with word-processing documents.

Our intention is to share tricks, techniques, problems, and other experiences that have helped or hindered users of our word-processing program, in order to assist members of the group with similar experiences.

Rather than formal training, which tends to overwhelm and lacks direct applicability, this group will be discussing and learning things of immediate value, making users more productive and efficient.

Please use the attached form to sign up the people in your department who you think would most benefit by this training. These people will be invited to join our group. Before each session, we will send them and you the agenda for the upcoming meeting and notes from the last meeting.

Word-Processing Users Group Sign-up Sheet

Department: _____

Name	Title	Extension
_____	_____	_____
_____	_____	_____
_____	_____	_____
_____	_____	_____
_____	_____	_____
_____	_____	_____
_____	_____	_____
_____	_____	_____
_____	_____	_____
_____	_____	_____
_____	_____	_____
_____	_____	_____

> **Sample Memo on Word-Processing Users Group**
>
> DATE: [Insert]
>
> TO: Member
>
> FROM: Your name
>
> SUBJECT: Word-processing users group
>
> We are forming a word-processing users group for those people who spend a good deal of their time word processing. Your manager has selected you as a potential candidate for this group.
>
> Our intention is to share tricks, techniques, problems, and other experiences that have helped or hindered some of you, in order to assist members of the group with similar experiences.
>
> Rather than formal training, which tends to overwhelm and lacks direct applicability, this group will be discussing and learning things of immediate value, making your job easier and more productive.
>
> Please plan to attend our first meeting, to be held [insert the date, time, and location]. Bring your problems, questions, and word-processing concerns. If you don't have any, come prepared to help those who do and maybe to learn something new.
>
> This is your group, and you will determine what you'd like to have happen in future sessions. We can have formal training on various topics at these sessions, demonstrations, and group discussions. So be sure to be at this first and most important meeting to help plan our strategy for the meetings to come.
>
> If you have any questions about this group, please don't hesitate to contact me.

types of reports, and a couple of off-the-wall applications you didn't think could be done with a word processor. As people talk about what they do, pay attention to the various levels of expertise that prevail and keep an eye out for the person or two who can assist you in running these meetings in the future.

You will want to open up the meeting to questions and answers. This session should be at least half of the allotted time, perhaps 30 minutes, during which anyone with a problem can raise a hand. Call on a user to describe the nature of the problem. Then anyone with a solution should offer assistance. Your role is to play monitor so that everyone gets a chance to ask and answer questions, and so things don't get off track. If you feel that a problem or solution is particularly long-winded, or not helpful to the majority of the group, suggest that the interested people take it up off-line. Keep the questions coming, and if no answers are forthcoming, write the issues down and see if someone is willing to research them and bring answers to the next meeting. You should step in with answers only if there is no one else to do so. If the entire session turns into a question-and-answer period, with the secretaries asking questions of you, some of the value is lost. These people are the experts in word processing, and some among them should have better answers than you. If you always leap in, or if you let group members always turn to you (as some naturally will), then these experts will remain hidden and you're wasting resources as well as time.

Some issues may come up which are better addressed through a quick hands-on training session, a demo, or some other format. In this case, you (or better, your designated senior word processor) will have to prepare for and set up the next meeting. These special hands-on sessions provide added value when a particular issue arises that is of importance to a large percentage of the members. Examples include the release of a new version of your word processor or a new add-on utility.

During the meeting, designate someone to take notes so that questions, answers, and other discussion can be written up as minutes, as reference notes for attendees, and as valuable guides for those unable to attend. The agenda for the next meeting, along with the time and date, can be sent along with the meeting minutes or as a separate document (and reminder) closer to the meeting date.

To Do

- Send out executive training memos.
- Schedule executive training.
- Find out which secretarial tasks can be automated.
- Develop word-processing competency tests.
- Send out word-processing users group memo to managers.
- Set tentative schedule and meeting place for users group.
- Identify users group leader.

Chapter 16

News

Communicate!

In a small organization in which everyone is in one office and everything that happens is common knowledge, a newsletter published from your department would be overkill. If, on the other hand, you are in a large organization with a department that is removed from some of your clientele, a newsletter can serve many useful purposes:

- To provide an educational tool
- To announce new technologies
- To provide scheduling information
- To describe accomplishments
- To seek feedback
- To alert people to computer problems

If you determine that there is a need for a newsletter, and that you have the necessary resources to devote to this type of work, you'll want to take pains to ensure that the product you put out is of high quality and well read. Unfortunately, simply because you have the need to tell, your readers may not have the desire to listen. There are two driving reasons that people read a newsletter: to learn and to be entertained.

If you can satisfy your readers' needs, while meeting your own goals of getting the right information to the right people, you'll have a successful newsletter. So begin with your reasons for putting together this newsletter and determine why your readership will be interested. Then think about the product itself, how it should be packaged, how often it should be delivered, and what the recognizable features will be.

You're the computer expert, so perhaps your newsletter should be high tech. Maybe you should distribute it on disk or via an electronic bulletin board. If it works, if it will be read, go ahead. You will be judged by the physical product you produce, so take some time to design a package that presents you in a flattering light. It may be better to put nothing out than to produce a poorly printed page that no one will pick up to read.

To make sure that what goes into the newsletter meets all your criteria, you'll have to submit it to several editorial reviews.

Edit for Success

A newspaper article goes through several editing phases before publishing. One editor will check for facts, another for grammar, still another for how the copy will fit on the page. You may be lucky enough to have professional editors on staff, or you may be author, editor, and publisher combined. In either case, all articles should be carefully reviewed, with the following edits in mind.

1. *Readability.* The key to maintaining readership is remembering who your audience is and what your objective is. Narrow your focus until you can identify a single person in your organization who personifies your target audience. Write directly to this person. Different articles or regular columns may be targeted for different audiences (e.g., one for techies, another for management), but any one piece should be written with a specific audience in mind. Keep revising until you can answer these three questions:

    Who is it written for?
    What are we trying to get across?
    Why will the intended reader read it?

2. *Jargon.* Get rid of it or explain it. It will be better to leave this job to a nontechnical person who can more readily identify what will appear as gibberish to other nontechnical people.

3. *Facts.* Have someone double-check any facts, prices, dates, titles, and spelling of people's names.

4. *Political correctness.* The most common error is sexist language, but offensive language or imagery of any kind will at a minimum cost you readership.

5. *Grammar and spelling.* Check carefully. People notice.

Editing Checklist
The target audience is:
The objective is:
Readers will be interested because:

Checkpoints:
  Readability
  Technojargon
  Facts, dates, names
  Political correctness
  Grammar and spelling

All the News

The topics your newsletter covers will depend on what's going on in the computer world, within your organization, and among your staff. For sources of organizational information, tap into the various committees to see what is going on that will interest your readers. Serve as your readers' guide to the technical world at large. What are some of the trends that employees will want to know about? Keep the newsletter in mind when reading trade magazines or attending shows and seminars. Keep a clippings file.

Regular columns provide continuity and create loyal readers who are interested in certain areas. Here are some possible areas of interest:

1. *Computers at home.* The more people use computers at home, the more disposed they will be toward computers at work. Help them at home, and you help the organization.

2. *Tutorial.* Keep people up to speed on jargon. Explain a new technology.

3. *Questions and answers.* Put frequently asked questions in print and forestall future calls to the help desk.

4. *Changes in policy or procedures.* Explain or restate company policy with respect to any number of computer issues—piracy, backups, personal usage, and so on.

5. *Corporate applications.* Here's your chance to blow your horn. What things are going on in the organization that are a result of your management? The headline may read "Inventory Reconciliation Department Switches from Spreadsheets and Saves Thousands" or "Disaster Recovery Plans Have Us Covered." Be careful to make the applications interesting, or people will begin to see the newsletter as an advertisement and stop paying attention.

You should also include stories from and about your readership; people enjoy reading about themselves. Publish regular schedules of classes, workshops, and committee meetings. Finally, consider adding cartoons just to keep it light.

Scheduling

In order to get even one issue out the door, never mind several over the course of a year, you will need to assign an editor, and your editor will need to start at once with a calendar. Work backward from the distribution date.

Distribution date

Publication date

Date to printer

Final layout date

Revisions due

Article submissions due

Article assignments

It is easier if you have established columns or topics that will appear in each edition. You can then assign space and responsibilities for these topics to different people. Allow enough time before publication for various edits and rewrites.

Your publishing schedule will depend on the size of your staff and your organization. Once a week is too frequent no matter what your size. And if you don't have the resources to put a newsletter together at least twice a year, it is probably not worth the effort. Monthly or quarterly is the most common schedule.

Survey Your Readers

By surveying your readers from time to time, you can better ensure that the newsletter is valuable to them.

The *Quarterly Byte* Annual Survey

Name (not required):   Date:

How regularly do you read the *Quarterly Byte*? (circle one)

  Cover to cover with enthusiasm

  Skim it mostly

  Rarely read it

  Run the other way when I see it coming

Why?

I would like to receive the *Quarterly Byte* (circle one):

                Less often   Same   More Often

The *Quarterly Byte* helps me:

The column I enjoy the most is:

The column I least enjoy is:

I would find the *Quarterly Byte* more useful if:

I would like to see (more) coverage on the following topics:

Other comments or suggestions:

Please return to the help desk by March 18.

To Do

- Assign an editor the task of scheduling.
- Determine appropriate design.
- Establish publishing schedule.
- Establish required budget.
- Create edit checklist.
- Settle on regular columns and contributors.
- Schedule first survey after 6 months.

Part

5

Performance Issues

Chapter 17

Hard-Disk Maintenance

If the CPU represents the brain of your computer, the hard drive is its personality. If your computer is an information bank, your hard drive is the bank's safe, holding all that's valuable. While every other aspect of the computer is an exchangeable commodity, a disk loaded with data is the single most differentiating feature, and therefore the most valuable aspect, of any computer. It is to these data repositories that we turn first when examining performance issues.

You will want to audit each and every hard drive on a regular basis. Your primary concern will be to detect any problems which could later cause data corruption. Your next concern will be to eliminate performance problems and establish an efficient environment. Initially you will want to audit every disk, and upon completion of the audit set a date for the next review. Some disks should be checked monthly; others, quarterly. At a minimum hard disks should be check twice per year—once during the annual PM checkup and again as a part of your disk audit.

Conventions

You are responsible for all the hard drives in your organization. The more similar they are, the easier your job will be. Some simple standards will help.

1. *Drive types.* If possible, standardize on one or two drive types. While the capacities of the drives can vary, keeping a standard drive type will simplify troubleshooting and support, and make swapping possible.

2. *Operating system.* Whenever possible, standardize on the operating system and the version as well, since this will eliminate cross-platform problems.

3. *TSRs and other utilities.* Memory management, disk caching, and other utilities should all be set up the same way whenever possible.

4. *Menu systems.* While not everyone has the same menu offering, the menu or shell system should be as consistent as possible from user to user so that you will know how to direct users quickly when they call with a problem. A combination of batch files, a menu program, windows, or some other interface should be used to achieve consistency.

5. *Standard directories.* Set up standard directories, all named identically, to minimize the time you need to track information down. A few common directories might be:

    \BATCH: Store all your batch files here for easy access.

    \DOS: Store all operating system files in this subdirectory.

    \TEMP: Set up a directory which will store files temporarily and which can always be disposed of. This avoids making other temporary directories with files that may be confused with important files later on, cluttering up your disk.

    \SYS: Set up a directory to house backup copies of your AUTOEXEC.BAT, CONFIG.SYS, and other startup files in case the ones in the root directory become corrupted or written over. (These files should also be kept on your boot disk so you're protected in the event that the hard disk becomes unbootable.)

6. *Separate data.* Data should be housed in subdirectories rather than with the applications program. Don't allow users to store spreadsheets with the program, or data files with the database manager itself. Keeping programs and data separate will make disk maintenance and support easier for the users and you.

7. *Floppy disks.* Floppies will be with us for a while as a storage medium, but for all the convenience they represent, they are tough to manage properly. Setting standards can help. Choose reliable brands that have their capacity clearly marked on the label, and stick to them. Preformatted disks eliminate enough problems to usually more than pay for the added cost. Don't have users buy their own disks. Buy in bulk and establish an inventory for users to draw from. Standardized drive types will save you and users many headaches, but if you have a mixed population of different density drives, label them clearly. If people are formatting their own floppies, each

diskette label should identify what CPU number it was formatted on. This will help you track a floppy drive that's out of alignment, because the floppies it formats won't be readable by other machines. Also note the capacity of the floppy (1.44 Mbytes, 360 kbytes, etc.), the owner of the floppy, the contents of the floppy, and whether it was transferred using a utility that will be required to get the information off the disk. A sequence number and total number of disks will help locate all the necessary disks later. Finally, indicate the date the copy was made.

```
F\CPU#101  1.44MB-KHE
           Berry & Lewis Files
           Fastback 2.0 1 of 4
           10/10/94
```

Disk Audit Procedures

During an audit, you will collect information regarding adherence to conventions as well as run diagnostics and performance-tuning software. When you are ready to schedule the audit, call the primary user of a workstation to set up an appointment, and request that the user perform a backup before you arrive. Always check the backup before you begin to make sure it exists and was done properly. You will also need to briefly explain to the user what is going to happen. Get the following preliminary information:

1. How often does the machine get turned on and off? "Once per day," "several times per day," "only on Friday," and "never off" are the most likely responses. You will have to settle in your own mind whether to advise people to turn off their machines or leave them running. The proponents of the "never off" school will say that the most stress to the system comes from turning it on and off, and that the resulting fluctuating internal temperature endangers sensitive chips. These arguments have merit, but the arguments in favor of turning a system off each night are just as compelling: By turning the machine off each night, you ensure a clean boot in the morning so that the backup of your system area is refreshed at least daily, and it's the green thing to do.

2. What are the most frequently run programs? You will want to set the order of the PATH in the AUTOEXEC.BAT and use this information to sort the disk during your optimization runs.

3. Has the primary user prepared a complete directory listing? If possible, supply the user with a tool that will print out the tree struc-

ture with subdirectories. Ask the user to review this list and to cross off any files that he or she wishes to archive. The backup should be done before you or the user proceeds to archive files. Tell the user to leave this directory listing for you or to send it to you for review. Let the user know approximately how long the audit will take and point out that you will have to have complete use of the machine.

Before the audit, pull the information (if any) from the most recent audit to review and have with you. Begin a new audit form with the date of the audit and the date of the last audit, your name, and the CPU number of the disk you are auditing. Note whether the drive is a local drive or server, the drive type, the capacity, and the operating system and version used. Also note the age of the drive. Older drives need to be watched more closely, and as you gather statistics on drive failures, you may want to establish an automatic replacement date rather than wait for the crash to retire each one. If there is any history of problems with this drive, now is the time to look for patterns or trends.

When you arrive for the audit, you'll have your bag of tools. A disk analyzer will give you the basic information you need, such as the contents of the CONFIG.SYS and AUTOEXEC.BAT, what cards have been installed, what interrupts are being used, and the drive type. You may find that no one product gives you all the information you need, but these tools are relatively inexpensive and will save you enough time to make it worth getting more than one. Sniffer, CheckIt, and System Sleuth are three such utilities.

Internal checks

At the start of the audit, ensure that the backup was properly run. Mark the backup as an archive for safekeeping in the event that an important file is deleted. Then look at what the primary user wants to archive. Also look the directory over for *.BAK type files, very old files, and very large files. Ask about these specifically. Can you get rid of them, archive them, or compress them? You'll want to get rid of as much extraneous or obsolete data as possible before you begin performance tuning, so that the new holes created by your deletions will be subsumed.

Take a look at the TSRs (Terminate and Stay Residents) being loaded. You will have to disable them before running any performance-tuning utilities. Are any of the conventional TSRs missing? Are unnecessary TSRs being loaded?

What kind of data compression techniques are being used? Programs like Stacker, which can double the effective storage capacity of your hard drive, should be noted. If the program is present, care should be taken that any analyzing tools or performance-tuning utilities do not corrupt these kinds of data. Consider the performance implications of any other commands in the startup files, like AUTOEXEC.BAT and CONFIG.SYS.

How much disk space is currently occupied? When a disk is full beyond 80 percent of its capacity, it's time to think about compressing, archiving, or moving to a bigger disk. Overfull disks become slower and are more likely sources of problems.

Is this a self-parking drive? If it is an older drive, it may not automatically park on shutdown. If this is the case, it is a good time to make sure that the appropriate parking utility is included in one of the PATH directories. (Parking utilities are not interchangeable among different systems, so don't mix and match.) Place a warning label on the outside of the machine: DO NOT MOVE THIS MACHINE WITHOUT PARKING FIRST! As newer machines predominate, people are less inclined to know about parking and will pick up any machine and move it without thinking twice. You will also want to include the PARK command on your main menu so that it is easy for anyone to run. Likewise, if the drive is self-parking, make sure there is no parking software loaded. Running this utility on self-parking drives can cause damage.

External review

Check out the environment in which the hard drive must operate. What's the ambient temperature? What's the temperature on the inside of the machine? What does the disk drive you have installed rate for? If too much heat is building up in the machine (how much is too much?), it might indicate an underutilized power supply or a failing power supply fan. Either situation will cause damage to drive components (not to mention the rest of the machine). Check to make sure there is enough air circulating around the vents and guard against widely and quickly fluctuating temperatures.

What else is around you? Put your hands and arms flat on the table with the PC (or your feet on the floor if that is where the PC stays). Are there noticeable vibrations? Even slight constant vibrations can cause hard-drive damage and promote chip creep, in which chips that aren't surface-mounted work their way slowly out of their sockets. If you notice a vibration, consider it significant. Even if you don't but the machine is near loud equipment, you may want to protect the drive by placing it on a vibration-absorbing pad.

Is the ambient air overly moist, smoky, or dusty? These environmental factors are corrosive to disk drives. Take any steps possible to reduce or eliminate their impact upon the drives.

Electromagnetic interference will cause data loss as well as intermittent trouble with monitors and printers. Some innocuous-looking office equipment can be an unwitting source of the problem. Look around for copiers, electric pencil sharpeners, fans, air conditioners, or other large electric motors. The farther these appliances are removed from the computer, the less likely they are to do damage.

The hard drive

Now start looking at the way the hard drive has been organized. Are the requisite, standard directories in place? Does the installed DOS version match the organizational standard? Do the batch files in \STASH match the copies on the root directory?

Take a look at the AUTOEXEC.BAT file. Does it automatically check for bad sectors and cross-linked files? Catching these immediately will reduce the likelihood of permanent file damage, so make the check routinely upon startup. Is there a utility such as MIRROR that will back up your system files to another area of your disk? This needs to be refreshed often to be helpful, so it too belongs in the AUTOEXEC. Of course, neither precaution is useful unless the machine is rebooted on a fairly regular (e.g., daily) basis. If the two systems are not in place, correct them. These utilities store the boot sector, FAT table, and root directory image for backup purposes.

Before you run any performance-tuning utilities, remove all TSRs and caching utilities, make sure that you have a full backup of the drive on hand and that your spare boot floppy is up to date. Your boot floppy should have on it the hidden system files, COMMAND.COM, AUTOEXEC.BAT, CONFIG.SYS, and files required by these startup routines, and the batch directory. Now you're ready to start some performance-tuning utilities.

Running a diagnostic like CHKDSK or Norton Commanders Disk Doctor will help uncover any problems that should be fixed immediately. Scan the disk and ensure that there are no problems before continuing.

There are many performance-tuning tools that handle most if not all the necessary procedures. You will want to compress the data on the disk by moving the files up to the front of the disk and the free space to the rear. You will also want to defragment the disk so that all your files are contiguous. These two procedures are usually done simultaneously. You will want to renew and restore the low-level format (in nondestructive mode, not by using FDISK!) to remagnetize the surface of the disk. Over time, this force is depleted and will eventually lead to data loss. Finally, you will want to sort the directories so that the most frequently used areas of the disk are toward the front. This will result in faster

Hard Drive Audit Form	
Date:	CPU number:
Local drive:	Shared drive:
Auditor:	Last audit:
Operating system:	Version:
Drive type/model/capacity/age:	
AUTOEXEC.BAT, CONFIG.SYS (print and attach):	
Verify backup (attach backup log):	
Copy startup files to \SYS:	Refresh boot floppy:
TSRs loaded:	
Caching programs used:	
Compression techniques used:	
Is this a self-parking drive?	
What parking software is included?	

Is heat a problem?
  Temperature outside cabinet
  Temperature inside
  Recommended temperature for drive
  Night temperature
  Circulation around machine
  Power supply fan	

Is the drive protected from vibrations and impact?
 	
Is there danger from magnetic fields?
  X-ray equipment
  Magnets
  Electric motors	

Are disk management conventions being adhered to?
  \BATCH
  \DOS
  \TEMP
  \SYS	

Does AUTOEXEC have automatic backup of systems area? When was this done? _____ Does AUTOEXEC have automatic check for bad sectors and cross-linked files?	

Hard Drive Audit Form (Cont.)

How often is this machine turned off?
  Frequently enough to refresh system area backup?
  More than once per day?

Does PATH command list directories in the order of most frequent access? If not, re-create.
Reboot without TSRs:
Run disk analysis (attach reports):

Run performance-tuning utilities (attach reports):
  Renew and restore low-level format
  Compress free space to end
  Defragment
  Sort directories
  Interleave (NA for IDE drives)

Reboot with TSRs and caching:
Available disk space: _____ percent
Comments:
Date of next audit:

startup and processing of these more frequently used applications. For non-IDE drives, you will also want to check the interleave factor to ensure that it is at the most efficient setting. These things should significantly speed up a machine that hasn't been tuned recently, and at the same time reduce the potential for nonrecoverable problems.

Following this performance tuning, reboot the machine and load all the normal operating TSRs. Now you're ready for the next machine.

When you review the data from this audit, you should be able to make recommendations to the primary user for ways to more efficiently use the hard drive, give a statement as to the overall health and future capacity of the drive, and make recommendations for the future. You should also set the next audit date, usually in 6 months to a year.

The audit, analysis, and report should take under 3 hours. If done annually, the procedure will prove to be a small investment for the increased speed and integrity of the hard drive.

Use a hard-drive audit form (see pages 175–176) to gather the necessary information. When entered into a database, this information will provide you with useful comparisons among different disks.

To Do

- Create list of each workstation with a hard drive.
- Create standards for disk management.
- Create disk management audit forms.
- Schedule audits.
- Set up database to house results and schedule follow-up.
- Report to user.
- Create reports to show overall trends and patterns.
- Analyze implications of organizationwide audits.
- Make recommendations to Security Committee.

Chapter 18

The Basics

The Three R's

Once you've addressed the physical and logical management of files on a disk, it is time to take a look at how users are using the tools at their disposal. While there are as many different ways to use a computer as there are computer users, there are some common applications that exist on every workstation. Database managers help with record keeping, word processing assists with writing chores, and the spreadsheet applications show up anywhere people are doing number crunching. The three R's in the computer world are *records, riting,* and *rithmetic.* Because these tools are so widespread, we'll look at each in turn to see how they may be better managed for improved performance.

Document Management

As a systems manager, you face an uphill battle in trying to get users to keep their disks clean and organized. Like the parent trying to regain control of a teenager's room, you confront dirty laundry at every turn. You may be tempted to shift the burden of this mess onto the user, hoping that, like communism, slobbism will eventually collapse under its own weight.

Chaos theory

With larger disk capacities and lower storage costs, it may seem wiser (and certainly easier) to expand rather than clean up, but conservation of disk space is only one of the reasons to consider implementing more formal document management policies. If you could perform a time study on the hours that people in your organization spend looking for haphazardly stored documents over the course of a year, the cost might astound you. Do an informal, random survey. Ask 10 people on staff how much time they spend in any given month searching for documents they or someone else has stored on disk. Also ask how often their searches are unsuccessful, and what the ramifications are of lost documents. Whatever number you get, you can be sure that it will grow as documents, people, and disk space grow within your company.

If wasted space and time don't bother anyone, there are still some serious considerations with respect to revision management. If someone who is unable to find the original document retypes a contract or proposal, there are now two originals of the same document. If later someone finds the original and makes changes to it, anyone working with the second original will not have access to the changes. The results can range from irritating to illegal.

Without formal document management policies, documents will be filed in the author's disk space, using the author's methods (or lack thereof). If this procedure works well in your organization, don't change it. In many situations, however, the approach will become unmanageable over time. Even if everyone is organized and thoughtful in document management methodology, the differences in approach will lead to problems. Many other questions need to be raised: Who will archive or delete old documents, using what criteria, and how? How should revisions be indicated? How will someone locate all the files that pertain to a specific subject? If these questions are difficult to answer, then they beg a standard document management policy, and in your role as systems manager you can help develop methods that work to the advantage of all. People will inevitably grumble, but they may secretly appreciate your efforts.

Document analysis

To develop a document management strategy that fits your constituents' needs, you'll need to analyze the types of documents that are being created. Since each department may have different needs, you'll need to investigate each independently.

To begin with, you will have to determine the various document types that are being worked on in the department: memos, client correspondence, sales contracts, newsletters. Each document type has different characteristics and different management needs. A document analysis form will help you proceed.

Document Analysis Form	
Department: *Sales*	Date: *January 10, 1994*
Document type: *Contracts*	
Description: *Sales contracts for custom-built engines*	
Who creates these documents? *Sales reps (10)*	
Volume? *1 per month per sales rep—10 per month average*	
Who may modify this document? *Legal, engineering, sales*	
Who else reads this document? *Scheduling, purchasing, management*	
How are revisions handled? *When a contract is modified, it requires a new contract number that must be logged and have authorized signatures.*	
Are old revisions needed? *Yes. Sometimes we go back to an earlier revision.*	
Are there security issues? *Not within the company*	
How are these documents filed now? *By client name*	
Are there other ways you'd like to search or sort? *Machine-class type, part number, contract number*	
How long do these documents stay active? *Depends on the contract length—usually 6 months to 1 year*	
When they are no longer active, what happens? *They need to be accessible for 6 years. Then they can be thrown out.*	
Are there any legal implications surrounding these document types? *Yes. They are legal contracts. Also, because of the nature of our business, they need to be available for audits for up to 6 years.*	

From the two sample document analyses (above and on the next page), you can see some of the issues that arise and how they vary from document type to document type. The sheer volume of documents being created will in part determine whether a document management strategy is called for. While some companies create relatively few documents during the course of business, others will create hundreds or thousands of documents daily.

Document-sharing requirements are also indicative. Particularly when more than one party may be modifying the same document, docu-

Document Analysis Form	
Department: *Sales*	Date: *January 10, 1994*
Document type: *Sales correspondence*	
Description: *Letters sent to prospects prior to sale*	
Who creates these documents? *Sales reps, sales secretary (11)*	
Volume? *10 per week per sales rep—400 per month average*	
Who may modify this document? *Sales*	
Who else reads this document? *Management*	
How are revisions handled? *Not applicable*	
Are old revisions needed? *Not necessary*	
Are there security issues? *Not within the company*	
How are these documents filed now? *It is up to the sales rep. Secretary files a correspondence file copy chronologically.*	
Are there other ways you'd like to search or sort? *Prospect name, type, date, sales rep*	
How long do these documents stay active? *No formal policy; not long*	
When they are no longer active, what happens? *They can be deleted.*	
Are there any legal implications surrounding these document types? *No*	

ment management policies need to be clear. All parties involved need to know where to find the latest revision, and what naming conventions to use. On the other hand, if there's a one-to-one relationship between author and file, a more relaxed atmosphere can work. Likewise, as revision, security, and legal issues arise, so does the need to establish standard practices. The same document management policy that works for sales correspondence may lead to lawsuits if applied to sales contracts. By completing these forms for each document type, you will ascertain how formal or lax your own company's policy needs to be. Further, you may determine that while some departments can be left on their own, others need to be reined in.

Document management options

The three main areas of document management are storage, retrieval, and disposal. At a minimum, therefore, document management policy must address where documents will be kept, how they will be retrieved, and when they will be deleted.

The most rudimentary method is a lax but legitimate attempt to standardize file naming and storage procedures. Here are some examples of these types of policies.

1. *File-naming conventions.* All documents pertaining to clients must have file names that contain the client's code. All hard-copy records must show the path and file name of the document in the lower-right-hand corner. (Word-processing macros can be set up to do this.) All file names use the author's initials as the first three characters.

2. *Storage procedures.* All correspondence will be stored on each user's local drive in a directory called \CORR. (This will make sharing of documents difficult.) All client files will be stored on the server in subdirectories by client code under G:\CLIENT\. (This may create security problems.)

3. *Archival policy.* All files that have not been modified in 6 months will be archived. Archived files will be deleted in 2 years. (Make sure there are no legal implications in this type of approach.) Each user is allocated 20 Mbytes filing space. The employee is expected to purge files as necessary so as not to exceed this space. (You'll have to determine when additional space is required.)

The main purpose behind standardized file names and locations is to facilitate retrieval of the document. With a limited number of characters, it can be very difficult to come up with a naming convention that is both standard and meaningful. Stamping hard copy with the path and file name makes it easy to retrieve a document for modification, but if you are searching for all the files that have to do with a certain project, or client, you may have a tough job ahead. Storing copies of documents in several places, as is done with paper files, can lead to version control catastrophes.

Usually archives are stored in order of the archive date, but in other cases archives may be made on a client or job basis. Are archives removed using tape or disk backup? A copy of the operating system and version of the backup system must be available if these archives are ever to be restored. (Keep this in mind when you're upgrading operating systems or backup utilities.) Some archive systems store optical snapshots of the documents, automating the microfiche operation. These documents can be retrieved for viewing, but cannot be modified or reused. In considering what archival system to implement, think of how you may want to retrieve those documents. After all, if you are never going to have to retrieve an archived document, there is no need to archive. Where should you store archives? Is one copy of your archives sufficient, or is an off-site copy required? When should archives be taken? When disk space fills up? Every year? When a job ends? The simpler the system, the easier it will be to manage. So if a floppy copy system works, there is no need to build a massive archiving system.

A more formal approach to document management will usually require a software interface. If during your document analysis you uncover the need for stronger tools, then you'll want to evaluate these products to determine which most closely fits your needs. Software products offer some tremendous advantages over the less automated approach. First of all, they force the users to adhere to the standards you set. The degree of adherence is established upon installation. Security can be established so that only some users can view or modify some types of documents, created by some subset of other employees. Version control can be implemented, and the archive process automated. Documents can be checked out for revision, and other users can be prevented from modifying those checked-out documents. Most helpful to users is the searching capabilities of these systems. In seconds, all the documents on all servers can be searched for key words. Full-text searching is facilitated as well. The rigidity of these enforced systems can seem like a straitjacket to laxer individuals, but if the advantages outweigh the impositions, the systems will be accepted and even applauded eventually.

Whether or not you formalize the document management process, someone needs to be designated as the document manager. In the absence of any other designation, this role falls to you. If you don't help the users deal with the issue of document management, you'll be forced to come to grips with it sooner or later as disks become cluttered and full, and you need to archive or expand. As with most of your responsibilities, you can proceed in a proactive or reactive way.

Spreadsheets

The automated spreadsheet is probably the most ubiquitous electronic tool after the word processor. It's there because it's useful. In the same way that the word processor helps people work with written communications more easily, the spreadsheet is the most valuable tool since the calculator in helping people to manipulate numbers. Since number crunching is such an integral part of business, it's not surprising that the electronic spreadsheet is showing up everywhere.

The problem is that spreadsheets can be underutilized, overutilized, or misused, resulting in small fortunes being wasted each day throughout organizations, in the form of wasted time and erroneous reports. There are applications that still cry out for a spreadsheet approach, and there are applications currently in a spreadsheet format that have no business being set up as such. Another problem with the electronic spreadsheet is the need to verify its reliability. In a manual spreadsheet, problems are less likely to occur, since we are forced to calculate each formula by hand. Further, problems that do result are more obvious. In an electronic spreadsheet, it is not only easier to introduce gross errors but also harder to spot them.

Because spreadsheet applications are so widespread and carry inherent problems, you will want to keep an eye on the current and possible uses for your spreadsheet products. Make sure that they are used in the right situations and are used correctly. Let's look at each of the types of problems, how to uncover them, and how to eradicate them.

Look for the clues

How do you find an application that should be but hasn't yet been introduced to the electronic spreadsheet? Spreadsheets are for manipulating numbers, so look for the numbers. While the situation points automatically to the accounting department, you'll also find applications in some unlikely places. Watch for the people who are always pecking away at the calculator or adding machine on their desk. Who's ordering the green columnar paper? You may find that the shipping clerk is still using a tabular format to calculate shipments to different zones by different methods. The sales department may still be calculating quantities and dimensions by hand. Maybe the secretary is tracking time on a columnar pad to call in to payroll each week.

Reel them in

An easier way to locate these applications is to draw the target audience to you. Your newsletter may do this, by informing users that there is an easier way. Give examples so users can visualize how an application might work for them, and help them make the connection between your example and their situation. Have a contest that encourages employees to spot the application in their area that would benefit most from computerizing. Have roundtable discussions among work groups, focused on finding out where time is being spent needlessly. Set up classes, and have people bring in their manual systems for automation. Offer a bonus reward for the application that saves the most time.

You'll have to be creative, because there are reasons that people don't come forward to suggest that an application is ready for spreadsheet automation. First, they may not know it is a candidate. Second, even if they know it can be done, they may prefer the tactile security of manipulating the numbers manually. There is something to be said for this too. When new numbers appear magically every month, and there are increasingly more numbers every month, employees may tend to look at the numbers less and less. By working numbers out, people become intimately familiar with them and may actually feel more responsible for them. So don't be too quick to pooh-pooh those who say they'd rather do it by hand. Many one-column check sums aren't worth computerizing anyway.

There will also be some outright fear of automation. That is, if a job that now takes one person 8 hours every month to complete can be turned into a 5-minute report through automated methods, what becomes of that person's job? This will not be a spoken fear, but it's very real nonetheless. Fortunately, most people are interested in doing their jobs in the most efficient manner possible. They rightly see that no matter how much time is saved, there is always more to be done if they are open to it.

These are some of the reasons that applications don't spring to the fore as possible candidates, and you will have to ferret them out by means of your department reviews and other investigatory means.

Coaching

When you find an application that warrants spreadsheet usage, don't just jump in and create the spreadsheet. Instead, provide the necessary coaching to enable the employee responsible for the application to create and manipulate the spreadsheet. If employees have no familiarity with spreadsheets, an introductory course or the tutorial will clear up some of the more rudimentary problems that arise when people are handed a tool without the proper introduction. Use this first application as a learning tool. Show students the basics and then have them work on the spreadsheet to try and come up with the necessary results. When they've completed their first attempt, go over the results. Give them credit for what they have accomplished, and then show them what they can do to improve the original.

Checking the spreadsheet

Check any formulas to see how the various summaries were obtained. Some people will catch right on to formulas and functions; others will miss the idea entirely. Don't be surprised to find spreadsheets for which totals, averages, and other complicated functions have to be worked out on a calculator and then keyed into the proper cell. Show the user the shortcuts.

The Medusan spreadsheet

The other extreme can be just as problematic. There are spreadsheet gurus who will create macros of Medusan complexity, a sheet that becomes nearly impossible to alter or to audit. These will need to be broken down to simpler tasks, and probably reprogrammed using a standard language.

Many spreadsheet applications evolve into database applications over time. If the application deals with historic records, or if many sorts and reports are required, you're probably looking at an application that's better suited for a database environment. While there are spreadsheet pundits who will say (and probably rightfully so) that you can do anything in a spreadsheet that you can do in a database, it's like arguing that a screwdriver can do anything that a hammer can do: True but ridiculous.

Jack and the spreadsheet

Another, often related problem is the Jack-and-the-spreadsheet phenomenon. Little Jack starts with an innocent-enough-looking spreadsheet that grows bigger and bigger as time goes on. Jack keeps asking for more and more memory, and complaining that everything is taking longer and longer, until one day the situation gets completely out of control. To find the giant spreadsheets is easy. They're out there eating up disk space and choking memory when they're up and running. When you come across one, find out what it does and how long it takes to run. You'll know very quickly if it is a candidate for conversion.

Database Focus

Few things in your job are more satisfying than identifying a database application and setting up a pessimistic user with a tool that makes his or her life infinitely more manageable. The effort taps your creative juices, and makes you feel like the white knight you were hired to be.

But often you merely stumble upon these opportunities to be helpful. You need to know how to uncover them more methodically.

Tracking the database application

Spreadsheet applications are often frustrated database applications, and you'll uncover your share of these during your spreadsheet audits. Historic reports are the other big finger pointing toward database destinations. Ask during departmental interviews what weekly, monthly, quarterly, and annual reports are produced. You'll find not only what results are being requested, but how the data are manipulated. You may be able to shave hours or days off the time that staff has been taking to produce some regularly requested reports. Once the data have been stored in a way that is easily analyzed, stand back and watch the flood of requests for additional analysis.

Look in files and Rolodexes. Mailing lists and inventories are surprisingly often left as manual systems, or as word-processing lists that someone painstakingly maintains.

Should every historic record be stored in a database? Probably, because it really takes no more time to store it in a database than on paper, and once stored it can be analyzed, sorted, and changed more easily. If the record will never be needed for future analysis, then why is it being captured at all? There may be exceptions, but they are no doubt fewer than are currently taken. When you implement a database solution, keep in mind the sophistication of the user and his or her needs. Don't spend weeks designing a full-blown application for a simple database requirement.

Taming the wild database

Log every database system you come across or create. Keep a name and description on file in an inventory of in-house applications (a database system itself). Any information system being employed to store or manipulate organizational data should be kept track of centrally so that you can audit the system from time to time and ensure that any system that becomes mission-critical is not handled haphazardly. Many critical operations within a company have evolved from simple spreadsheet or database applications. If they are not logged and tracked, they live and die with their creator. This situation makes the organization that depends on such applications very vulnerable. What happens when the key person takes an extended vacation or, worse, leaves the company suddenly under not-so-friendly terms?

Once a database system has been identified, a regular audit of the system should be scheduled (see Chapter 12) to uncover any problems, improve performance, and ensure that the system is protected.

To Do

- Schedule document analysis meetings with each department head.
- Determine document management needs and establish policy.
- Schedule spreadsheet audits.
- Schedule database reviews.

Chapter 19

Departmental Focus

Three Blind Men

As in the story of the blind men examining the elephant, it is difficult to gain a full picture of your organization by merely examining one part or another. Whenever you look at one small component, as you do on a daily basis when dealing with support issues, you are likely to make the blind men's mistake of assuming that the whole is nothing more than an extension of the part you're faced with. Solutions that come from this type of analysis may well work for the part, but often fall sadly short of being satisfactory for the whole. On the other hand, you need to work with problems that you can get your arms around. Like the blind men, you are limited in your ability to grasp the entire picture, and must work with individual pieces of the puzzle to try to fit together a meaningful overview.

The departmental focus study attempts to break down the picture into meaningful, graspable pieces, while also tying the individual parts back to their composite whole. It is a functional, task-by-task analysis of the organization that helps you understand the world you are trying to support, and thereby be able to recommend improvements that address not only the pieces but the whole.

If the elephant could have talked, the blind men might have begun by asking for an overview. Your elephant does talk, and you can get this overview from the organization's mission statement. Learn as much as you can about the full mission of your organization, and its current goals, to obtain the broadest definition you need: a bird's-eye view of the elephant. From here, move from department to department, looking at the role and the long- and short-term goals of each. Then, within each department, look at the functions being performed, the tasks being carried out, and how automation may or may not play a role.

Today, many company computers are used for one or two applications. These tasks may have justified the initial investment, but often don't come close to utilizing the full potential of the machines. Companies can come closer to maximizing the return made on their investment by looking at what other tasks the machines can be made to do. The departmental focus study will help identify new uses.

Initial Meeting

Begin the departmental focus study by interviewing each department head. This person needs to understand and approve of what you will be doing in ensuing interviews, and will be the most interested in your results. An introductory memo may help smooth the way. Explain your purpose and how much time you'll need (30 minutes to 1 hour). Begin your meeting by asking the department head what he or she sees as the purpose of the department and the strategic goals that are currently guiding the allocation of resources within the department. Find out what his or her concerns are in general and regarding automation in particular.

Finally, determine what functions are being performed within the department, and which key personnel you should talk to about each function. Any function that has strategic links should be identified, along with a ranking. Suppose that during your interview with the head of customer service, you find that the department has two primary strategic goals:

- To improve customer satisfaction ratings (code CS)
- To cut the cost of call response (code CC)

If the department head feels that a particular function has very high implications for client satisfaction, its strategic rating might be CS1. A lower-priority function might be a CS3.

Time Study Analysis

Once you have identified all the functions of the department and key personnel associated with each function, it is time to begin gathering information from these sources. Again, you should arrange to meet for up to an hour with each person mentioned by the department head. You will want to collect information from key personnel on the tasks they perform (or that others perform under their direction) for each of the

Departmental Focus Study Overview	
Department name:	
Department head:	Phone:
Interviewer:	Date:
Mission of the department:	
Strategic short-term goals of the department:	
Short-term budgeting information:	
Strategic long-term goals of the department:	
Long-term budgeting information:	
Currently identified problems:	

Departmental Focus Study Overview (Cont.)			
Function:	Strategic Rating:	Key Person:	Phone:

primary functions listed for the department. If one person is associated with more than one function, take each function in turn and perhaps schedule different times to discuss the different functions. A letter of introduction from you or the department head should answer any questions people may have regarding the reasons for your visit. The letter may also be used to request some of the information up front. You might ask people to complete the preliminary functional analysis form and the function task list (see page 196), since these will require some preparatory thought and time.

You may meet with resistance in the form of "I don't have the time" or "There's not really much for me to explain." It's understandable that people don't want to make time for something that may just change their world for the worse. Why take the chance? The department head may be able to force it, but you'll get better results if people understand that you're interested in helping them. Try to initiate discussions with "What's your biggest headache when it comes to computers?" Point out that you may be able to eliminate this headache as a result of the study. A separate functional analysis form needs to be filled in for each function by the key person for that function.

In order to see which tasks are the most time-consuming, and which have the most impact on the strategic goals of the department or the

Preliminary Functional Analysis Form

Department:

Function:

Key person: Phone:

Interviewer: Date:

How many others are associated with this function?

Your biggest headache when it comes to this function is:

What percentage of your time is spent on this function?

Rate the importance of this function to the company from 1 (vital) to 5 (totally irrelevant), and explain your rating:

How are you using computers in this function today?

Problems, concerns, wishes, or comments regarding computers and this function:

Use the function task list to identify all the tasks that make up this function and fill out the cycle time.

---

company, the function task list delineates each task, the time it takes each week, and notes current automation status and problems.

In order to rank functions and tasks by the time resources currently consumed by them, you'll have to standardize your time elements. Ask questions that will uncover common problems, and note by each task which problems apply.

- Should this task take less time? (code TC)
- Are the same data entered twice? (code DD)
- Is accuracy a problem? (code AC)
- Other problems?

In determining how much of the task is currently automated you can code each task as:

IM = Input manual
IA = Input automated
PM = Process manual
PA = Process automated
OM = Output manual
OA = Output automated

Common solutions may be suggested by the key personnel of various tasks. If there is more than one task problem that might be solved by a particular technology, you'll want to make out a report that will show

Function Task List			
Task	Hours per Week	Computer Involved Today	Problem Solution Codes

all the benefits to be derived from the implementation of a common solution. Sample solution codes might be:

S1 = Wide area network
S2 = Scanning capacity
S3 = Desktop publishing capabilities

Results and Recommendations

The results of your analysis will be a report of your findings, with recommendations based on what new automation will create the biggest advancement toward departmental or organizational goals with the least amount of effort and resources.

To facilitate your analysis, this information should be entered into a database, and the records sorted by:

Time consumed

Strategic issue and rating

Common problems

Common solutions

Other things being equal, those tasks that take up the most time will bear more consideration than those taking less time. Likewise, those tasks related to strategically important functions carry more weight than other tasks.

Common problems and common solutions will help show how the impact of change in one area will positively affect many others. When the cost of a solution is weighed against the many problems it will solve, the investment may become obviously wise.

With all this as input, you'll want to make some long- and short-term recommendations. List each recommendation in the order you feel it should be implemented. Each recommendation should reveal:

1. The benefit that the recommendation will provide for the department or organization, and if possible the strategic goal(s) that it works toward.
2. Specific problems that it will address throughout the department, listing the various tasks that are pertinent. Be specific: If the recommendation will save time, how much time? If the recommendation will save money, how much money?
3. The implementation steps. What needs to happen in order to effect the recommended solution?

4. The time frame involved. How long will it take to implement the recommended solution?
5. Responsibilities. Who will be responsible for the implementation and ongoing results of your recommendation? This party needs to be identified before an assessment of the recommendation can be made.
6. Budgetary considerations. How much will it take to implement the recommendation? If you cannot fix a dollar value to the recommended solution, identify as many specific items as you can.

Begin your report with a summary, followed by details of your recommendations, followed by the analysis that led to your recommendations. This will be a management report, meaning that readers are likely to be more interested in your recommendations than in your data. Have the detailed backup to your recommendations but be prepared to discuss the issues from the top down.

Follow-up

Management will have to give you the go-ahead regarding which solutions to implement and which will wait or be discarded altogether. You may have to stay on top of these recommendations to ensure that they aren't put on a back burner until they're no longer current enough to be acted on. If possible, wrap all the departmental reviews into an organizational review for presentation to top management. With pressure from the highest levels, you're more likely to see action at the departmental level. It will be important to maintain the momentum of these recommendations if they are ever to move off the drawing board. If they are given the thumbs up, make sure they're in the budget. Then get them on the calendar and start making progress. At this point they become your concern, and among your goals for the year.

To Do

- Review organizational mission statement and goals.
- Get list of department heads.
- Send out memo to department heads regarding departmental focus.
- Meet and fill out departmental overview form.
- Send out memo to key personnel.
- Meet and fill out preliminary functional analysis form and function task list.

- Create functional analysis database and generate reports.
- Evaluate solutions and develop long- and short-term recommendations.
- Present report to upper management.
- Conduct follow-up until all recommendations are approved, put on hold, or rejected.

Chapter

20

Communications Focus

While the departmental audit focuses on the functions being performed in the various departments, the communications focus aims its attention on how information is passed among the different departments, and between departments and the outside community. Communications is the essence of data processing. Gathering, processing, and disseminating information is what it's all about. Therefore, we must be constantly looking to improve on the content and delivery of the information we provide. This chapter focuses on the delivery vehicle.

Data are probably passed around your organization right now in several different ways—over the telephone, through the mail, over modem and public access systems, via direct lines, across network connections, by fax, and floppy to floppy. In each of these cases, a decision has been made to use one form of communication over another. Is it the fastest, most efficient, safest method? Probably not, if no one has addressed the issue.

The first job of the communications subcommittee will be to map the paths of communication as they exist today, and in the process to gather feedback on any problems with the current setup.

The Communications Map

Each department should have its own map, within its location placed in the center of the map as a circle with lines of communication flowing in and out (Fig. 20.1). Arrows can be used to denote direction, and color coding can represent the method of communication:

Black—hard copy

Red—file transfer by floppy

202   Performance Issues

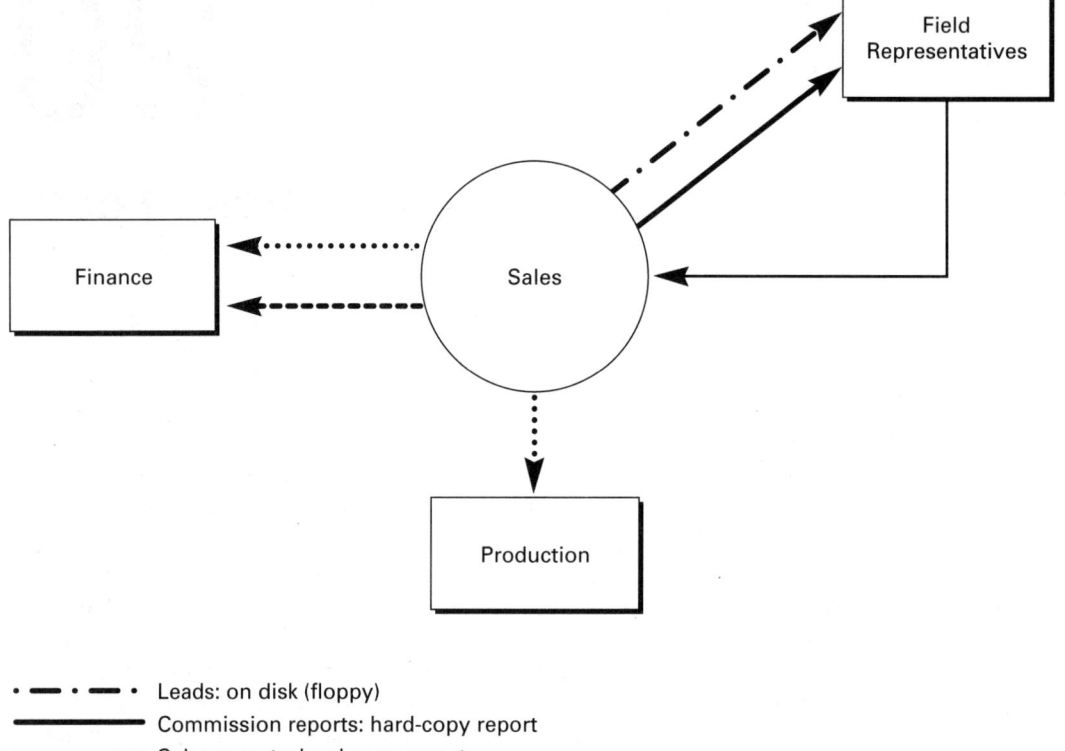

Figure 20.1 Communications diagram.

Orange—file transfer by modem over public access

Green—file transfer over direct line

Blue—file transfer over network connection

Other departments can be shown as squares. If some departments are located in other buildings or cities, show this separation graphically with the use of lines or colors. Other entities such as vendors, governments, and clients should likewise be identified.

Each arrow can be marked with a numeric identifier with footnote references. A companion table will show, for each line of communication, more detail regarding the type of data being transferred, the frequency of the transfer, and any problems that are currently identified.

The rendering of these communications maps will bring some of the most obvious problems and their solutions to light. Other issues may not become clear until all the maps are assembled and addressed as a whole.

The Ladder of Communication

When the communications subcommittee has completed the mapping process, the analysis can begin. One way to view all the communications links is to lump them by type of communication. If we think of the hierarchy of communications methods as a ladder, then on the bottom rung we have hard copy, and at the top rung direct connections. The primary consideration for each link that is made at one level of communication is whether there is a cost justification in moving to the next higher rung.

Beginning at the lowest, hard-copy rung, we may see, for example, that monthly reports are still submitted as hard copy by outside sales reps. Recognizing that they all now have laptops and the ability to connect to home base for leads and literature requests, it is a simple deduction to conclude that the benefits of having them submit reports on-line will speed up the information flow, and also eliminate the need to reenter data for further processing. In this case, they will skip the floppy transfer rung and go directly to modem transfer. Can they rise still further to direct connections? No, given the limited connection that any one representative is making from his or her own home office.

Each link is taken in turn to see how far up the ladder the task can be taken before cost justification runs out. There will be many tasks identified for which a local area network or other direct connection makes sense from the point of view of speeding up communication, but which cannot be cost-justified in its own right. These should be identified as such, because when looked at as a whole, there may be enough different benefits to justify the move. Direct connections to distant offices must be viewed in this way.

Wide Area Direct Connection Alternatives

At the higher rungs of the communications ladder there are several options that need to be considered. Once you have determined the need for this level of communication, you will have several options to consider. Direct lines to distant offices can seem dauntingly expensive, but there are ways to keep the costs down, and the alternative methods are probably less expensive than they first appear. By identifying all the areas that could possibly benefit from a direct connection, and by weighing the cost of alternative solutions, you will probably come out more clearly in favor of the direct connection.

When evaluating the costs of direct connections, you'll be faced with evaluating solutions that involve dial-up lines, leased lines, microwave, fiber-optic, and even satellite links. Dial-up lines are considered the least-cost solution, but when frequent, long-distance connections are required, the cost of a direct line can actually be cheaper. Direct lines create a permanent link, so no dialing is required, and move your data over the lines much faster than dial-up systems can handle. Depending on the speed of the throughput you require, you can choose between various categories of leased lines. T1 lines offer a throughput of 1.544 Mbits/second (your maximum dial-up capacity is about 50 Kbits/second), and T3 lines push that rate to 45 Mbits/second. This capacity is usually well in excess of what any one application will require, but when all the possible uses for a direct connection are taken into account, and because these direct lines can be split into several data and voice channels, they can be far cheaper than they appear at first glance. All the costs of the alternative solutions need to be weighed against the monthly cost of between $5000 and $10,000.

If even faster performance is necessary, consider fiber-optic cabling with throughput capacity of up to 100 Mbits/second. You may even be lucky enough to be in a city where such cabling is already available, or you may lay it yourself.

Microwave and satellite connections can be used to connect sites without physical connections. Microwave gives you the performance of a T1 line within a radius of a few miles. It eliminates your monthly service charge with a one-time cost, and the payback period is less than one year. Satellite links can carry you the distance, but performance can suffer.

Unless you are very familiar with the alternative technologies and vendors in your area, it will be better to put forth a request for quotation (RFQ) stating your needs, and allowing the various solutions to identify themselves to you. Be aware that because this is such a new and constantly changing technology, there are many new players being introduced, and you'll want one that can support you for the life of your communications needs. Consider the ability to provide satisfied references before and above the price tag with any vendor solution.

Application of New Technologies

Communications technology is one of the most rapidly changing areas, and the ramifications of these changes can be significant and sweeping. The communications subcommittee should overlap the new technology subcommittee in its role in this area, by helping to identify those new applications that may have a bearing on the current forms of communication. Some current examples:

Faxing. Who's faxing what now? What other faxing applications are there around? Should we be investigating fax board technology, faxing late at night, fax-back phone lines for clients?

Scanning. Where is data entry occurring now? What benefits would be derived from replacing the data entry with scanning technology?

The actual testing and evaluation of new communications technology may be handled by the new technology subcommittee, but the impetus can flow from the communications subcommittee, which is more finely attuned to the passing of information.

Departmental Recommendation

While the group will look at the communications alternatives, their costs and benefits from an aggregate point of view, at some point this must be dealt with on a departmental level. Review each departmental map and develop a recommendation for long- and short-term solutions for improving the performance of the communications that are currently taking place within that department.

To Do

- Establish the communications subcommittee.
- Develop communications maps for each department.
- Perform cost/benefit analysis of various connection technologies according to the aggregate needs of the organization.
- Create departmental long- and short-term recommendations.

Part

6

Strategic Issues

Chapter 21

New Technology Review

Catching the Wave

New technologies are constantly pouring over the horizon from theory into the realm of possible, and in some cases very quickly from there into every business and household—the answering machine and the facsimile machine are two recent examples. Some new technologies may have obvious application in your organization; others may be just as obviously unsuitable. There is also bound to be a sizable margin of products that are of questionable value, where an insightful eye might grasp a potential use unimagined by less creative minds. Herein lies the potential for uncovering real competitive advantage in the application of new technologies.

As the systems manager, you have the Sisyphean task of trying constantly to scale the mountain of information that continues to pile up on your desk regarding new technologies in the form of trade magazines, news releases, and advertisements. Trade shows, seminars, and product demonstrations are among some of the other channels by which this new information enters your world. You have to absorb as much of this data as possible, with an eye toward catching the wave when a particular new invention will reward your organization above and beyond the cost of introducing it.

If your organization is large, and the numbers of your direct staff sufficient, then you can split up the job into more manageable chunks. Assign one person as the watchdog for the accounting department, another as the lookout for marketing and sales, and so on. You can also divide the labor along technological lines—one of you is in charge of printing, another monitors, and the like—although there is a tendency for new technology to create new technical categories. Work-flow products, for instance, introduced a new category of software. Further, by concentrating your investigation along departmental or functional lines, you focus less on technology for technology's sake, but instead on its applied usefulness to an existing process or group of people.

Many companies are happy to let others break trail, joining only when the path is clearly marked and well traveled. To be poised to capture the wave, to be the first to make use of some new technology, requires a willingness to invest in the research and the trials and errors that necessarily follow. This is the price you must be willing to pay for the potential of competitive gains. Your budget and the other resources you may be able to draw on will be based on upper management's position on the risk/reward continuum. If there is no budget for large-scale research, there may still be room for ad hoc allocation of funds when a clearly obvious opportunity presents itself. In fact, whether it's stated or not, you are probably expected to identify these more obvious applications as a matter of course. If your organization is small, and you're an avid reader of trade magazines in your spare time, you may be able to handle this informal investigation on your own. If not, then establish a new technology subcommittee and let it help you stay on top.

The New Technology Subcommittee

The new technology subcommittee should have a representative for each department within the organization. Members can be your staff representatives or actual department staff, or a combination of the two. Your staff will have more up-front knowledge about the new technologies at the start, but the department staff will have a better understanding of the needs and focus of the department. The more important prerequisite for participation should be an interest in and excitement about new technology and the possibilities it brings. It won't take but one or two naysayers in the group to preclude the chances of any new technologies being introduced. There's a place for rational negative arguments, but at the preliminary stages, pessimism will only kill new ideas aborning.

The committee should meet once every month or two. Its goal is simple: to identify and test new technologies that have an appropriate application within the organization. The agenda will include discussions of new technologies, and progress being made on current evaluations of other new technologies.

When a member of the committee hears about a new technology that he or she feels the committee should investigate, it is put on the agenda with the sponsor's name associated with it. Each member should be encouraged to be a new technology sponsor at least once each year. The new technology sponsor, during the introductory meeting, should come prepared to provide the information described below.

New Technology Proposal

First, give a general description of the new technology. What are the primary features and benefits it has to offer? Concentrate on the need it may fill in the organization: Will it save time? Improve sales? Increase accuracy? Put pizzazz in presentations? Why should the company spend time and resources investigating this rather than some other idea?

If possible, give examples of how it might be applied in the organization. The real benefits, the best applications, may not become obvious until further on in your investigation, but unless you have some inkling of the possible advantages, or unless you have complete freedom to investigate technology for technology's sake, you won't get the necessary blessings (money) to investigate further.

Only the basic cost considerations should be identified at the preliminary stage. What is the purchase price? What are the installation, training, and support ramifications? A full and accurate cost analysis won't be possible but the idea is to get a general feel for the fiscal impact.

A new technology proposal, containing this basic information, should be developed by the sponsor and presented to the new technology subcommittee at the introductory meeting. The proposal shouldn't be long. The form shown here can be used to facilitate uniformity among proposals and easier evaluation.

After the introduction of a new technology, further discussion should be deferred until the next meeting to give each member of the committee time to review the proposal and to add his or her own input as to possible benefits, applications, and costs to be considered. When the committee reconvenes, any other benefits and costs should be added to the original proposal and a general discussion of the pros and cons should ensue.

One of the primary goals of this meeting will be to determine how an evaluation would have to be carried out in order to effectively determine the value of the new technology. Who should be involved, what would have to be purchased, and what should the goals and the milestones be? This will help the group come to a go/no-go decision

Strategic Issues

New Technology Proposal	
Date:	Sponsor:
Description:	
Why we should investigate further:	
Possible applications:	
Preliminary cost implications:	
Committee conclusion: Date:	

based on the perceived benefits and the costs involved in the evaluation process.

If it is decided not to pursue a topic, the group may suggest that at another time, or under different circumstances, the topic should be revived. If this is the case, discuss those scenarios under which you will reconsider the technology. The sponsor should take note for future reference.

New Technology Evaluation

If the group's decision is to go forward with the evaluation, then the evaluation plan needs to be formalized.

New Technology Evaluation Plan	
Date:	Sponsor:
New technology description:	
Goal of this evaluation:	
Milestones and responsibilities:	
Evaluation requirements and associated costs:	

If, for instance, you work in a bank and scanning technology has been proposed and approved for further evaluation, the associated forms might look something like the ones on page 214.

214 Strategic Issues

New Technology Proposal

Date: *2/15/95*   Sponsor: *Sandra Gilespi*

Description: *Scanner technology*

Why we should investigate further:

Time savings by eliminating the need to enter data filled in on forms

Reduction in errors from data entry mistakes

Possible applications:

Christmas Club

Customer service cards

Preliminary cost implications:

$1000–$5000 for necessary hardware

Committee conclusion: *Proceed*

Date: *3/15/95*

New Technology Evaluation Plan

Date: *4/15/95*   Sponsor: *Sandra Gilespi*

New technology description: *Scanner technology*

Goal of this evaluation: *To see if scanners could be used to reduce data entry time and errors*

Milestones and responsibilities:
  Kathy—Determine what the differences are between scanners.
  Kathy—Determine what types of scanners are appropriate for our applications
    (namely, Christmas Club and customer service)
  Kathy—Try to get evaluation model of three desirable scanners
  Kathy, Joe—Scan sample set of Christmas Club cards
  Kathy—Formal cost/benefit analysis
  Kathy—Results and recommendation to committee

Evaluation requirements and associated costs:

Time:
  Kathy—40 hours
  Joe—8 hours

Cost:
  No outlay required if we can get evaluation unit

Education

During the evaluation process you want to be educated, not sold, so be wary of involving sales personnel who represent a particular brand. Some reps, however, may be very helpful, comfortable in an education mode, and if you stumble onto these types, take advantage of their willingness to help. You will probably pick up information that you hadn't thought to ask about, but the committee as a group should help frame your investigation by asking many questions that can serve as milestones in the evaluation process.

One of the problems with new technologies is that descriptions go only so far. Until a person holds it in hand, or sees how it works, it is a vague concept at best. Getting an evaluation unit in will help the educational process take place, and further the ideas that the group may have about practical applications.

With questions in hand, get hold of the evaluation unit. You can usually borrow an evaluation unit from a company that makes the product. Such companies understand the need for this evaluation phase, but be prepared to return the product sooner than you'd like. For this reason, don't have too many new technologies under review, because you're going to have to take a look at each as a group and educate yourselves pretty quickly.

The sponsor should get the unit and play around with it, trying to answer the questions the group has posed already, and to come up with additional questions and possible uses. Plan a demo and a general, initial assessment for the next meeting.

Another brainstorming session should reveal additional possible advantages of incorporating this new technology, and a better idea of the possible pitfalls and problems should be developing.

Problems at this point should be put in the form of questions. It may be difficult to glean from one representative product whether the problems that arise from its use are problems with the product or with the technology itself. In the case of the bank scanner, a low-grade image or lack of character recognition may make members think the technology isn't applicable. Looking at more than one product can help eliminate these misconceptions.

Many new technologies that you look at will not go beyond the committee room meetings. Others, though, may have the potential of making giant progressive strides for the organization.

At the end of the evaluation process, the subcommittee will determine whether the new technology has merit, justifying the cost of introducing it, or whether it should be abandoned, at least for the time being.

Product Evaluation and Selection

If the technology is to be introduced, the issue of product evaluation and selection arises. This process can follow directly on the heels of the technology evaluation, or may be turned over to another team selected for that purpose.

The goals of the product evaluation team are:

- To determine what criteria should be weighed and to assign their weights relative to their importance for the company
- To select the possible products for evaluation and to measure each product against the evaluation criteria
- To recommend the most suitable product on the basis of testing and evaluation findings and to suggest the implementation strategy that will most successfully and smoothly introduce the new technology

The list of criteria should be gleaned from as many sources as wish to have input, and from every source where the data are available. Get feedback from all the departments or you will not have their cooperation when it comes to the implementation stage. Ask questions of vendors: Why is their product superior? What new features are planned for the next release? What should you look for in a product? Each vendor will have different responses and these can help you uncover some of the issues that differentiate the players. Check magazines for product reviews. Some of their criteria will match your own, some will be irrelevant, and some may cover issues that you haven't thought of yet.

There may be some criteria that can serve as minimum requirements for further consideration. Other issues may be important rather than critical, and still others will be merely desirable, or of minimal importance. Determine a rating scheme that will give more weight to the important features.

For the initial list of products be sure to include any products recommended by employees. Expand the list as needed by pulling from your own knowledge, trade magazines, and on-line searches. Too many products make the evaluation process unnecessarily long, but too few, particularly if you've left off somebody's favorite, will often come back to haunt you.

If you have minimum requirements, then the preliminary lineup of products should be tested for compliance in this area up front. Any product that cannot meet any of the minimum requirements should be eliminated. The finalists that emerge from this stage should all be measured against the remaining criteria, and given a raw score. This raw score should be weighted according to the importance of the criteria, and if scores are grouped into categories, the overall scores of the categories will need to be normalized.

During this process you may uncover additional criteria that should be included in the test list. Other issues may fall away as unimportant or impractical. Changes in the criteria should be approved by the evaluation team, and kept to a minimum.

When the scores are weighted and normalized, the result will hopefully be a clear winner: the product that most closely fits the needs of the organization. The recommendation will point to the important factors which led to the product's nomination, and should also include notes on how best to implement the new technology into the organizational environment.

Implementation

Will there be a test bed where the product is introduced and monitored before mass installations take place? Will there be additional training requirements that need to be taken care of before the first installation occurs?

Unless there are compelling reasons for mass introduction, the testbed approach offers the smoothest transition. Begin with the group that offers the least resistance, or the one that will reap the most benefit. Establish a time frame, from one month to a year, over which the test bed will be monitored for success and surprises which can be helpful in the initiation of other departments.

When New Technology Eliminates Jobs

There will be new technologies that come to light which have the potential of saving your organization a great deal of money in the form of payroll expense. How will your subcommittee deal with these issues? There is no job today which will not be obviated by machines at some point; not ours, not yours. Indeed, a principal cause of the growing global economic crises is the encroaching capabilities of the machine class. You and your new technology subcommittee are on the forefront making this possible. Like it or not, this places part of the responsibility for worker displacement squarely on your shoulders. In many cases, you will be removing the drudgery from someone's job and that person will be truly grateful. In other cases, you will take a process that took hundreds of labor hours and turn it into a 10-minute report kicked off at the press of a button each month. When a person's entire career was enmeshed in the creation of those reports, don't expect him or her to be thrilled by your new invention.

The hope for these displaced workers, and indeed for us all, is in our recognition that technology must be balanced with humanity. For every gain we make in efficiency and automation, we will need to make equal strides in service and customer satisfaction. If whenever we replace a task with a machine we think about how we can reuse the people power toward better service for our clients, we maintain the balance between technology and service. Service will be the hinge upon which your ultimate competitiveness swings, and people will always be at the heart of service.

To Do

- Set up new technology subcommittee.
- Schedule first meeting.
- Choose first new technology to investigate.
- Develop new technology proposal for presentation to new technology subcommittee.

Chapter 22

Setting Standards

The Needs of the Many

Standardization is a strategic decision. To even consider the implementation of a standard makes a strategic statement to the people within your organization: that the needs of the few may be superseded by those of the many. Standardization is a solution whose aim is increased efficiencies and economies, and no one can deny that there are benefits to be gained when instead of supporting five word processors, the company standardizes on one.

Your standards may be as gentle as a preference list, or as forceful as a no-exceptions mandate. There are good reasons and important ramifications that come out of standardizing, and the way you go about it, if you choose to go about it, will mean the difference between chaos and a smooth progression forward.

The Pros

The case for standardization is strong: First of all, the level of support needed to handle as many different products as personal preference dictates would be prohibitive. The fewer the number of word processors being used (and the fewer versions of each word processor), the easier it will be for your support team.

Communication between people and departments that speak different languages (I speak Microsoft Word, you speak WordPerfect, and there's probably a few Multimate diehards out there too) is frustrating. Conversions are time-consuming and often unsatisfactory. Training required when someone moves from one department to another and has to learn another product is expensive. Enhanced purchasing power is another justification. If, rather than buying 10 copies of 10 different products, you are purchasing 100 copies of a particular product, you will be able to get a site license, or volume discounts.

The Cons

On the other hand, there are some compelling arguments against standardization. A compromise, which is what the standard usually is, is by definition less than ideal. Personal preference is built on a comfort level, previous experiences, unique requirements, and possibly other factors that can't be dismissed as inconsequential. If there is no overwhelming economic benefit to be had, or efficiencies to be gained, as a result of data sharing, support, or training issues, then personal preference should rule the day.

The Ideal Candidate

The first and most obvious things to standardize are those ubiquitous and most basic of software tools that create files meant for sharing: word processors, spreadsheets, database managers. Hardware standards make the most sense for CPUs and printers, but grow from there. Begin where the justification is the strongest. Your support logs will show you how many calls are related to supporting multiple platforms. Your purchasing log will show you how many individual acquisitions of a similar type of hardware or software have been made. These numbers will help you determine whether there's a real economic benefit to be had. Your communications audit will reveal some of the gains in efficiency that might be derived from standard systems. If staff moves around frequently among departments that have different platforms, you have some impetus. If you see people requiring training on different products that perform the same function, you have an indication.

Justification

Let's say that your analysis indicates that a word-processing standard would save your organization thousands of dollars annually. Present your findings in the form of a recommendation to implement a word-processing standard and get the approval of upper management to perform a study. You may, without much formal data, be able to elicit an intuitive agreement that standardizing will benefit all in the long run. If your management is more numbers-oriented, you'll have to collect numbers pertaining to support calls, training hours, and purchase decisions.

The Task Force

Once you've been given the go-ahead, you'll have to put together a task force. This will be a small but representative group, usually one member from each department. If you limit your input by limiting the numbers in your task force, the resulting standard will be seen as an imposition on the many for the good of a few. In your first meeting you will have to explain to the group what their role and goals will be and ensure that everyone at the table is open to the possibilities and benefits of standardization in general.

Each member should then be directed to return to his or her own department, and to find out what are the currently used products, preferences, and problems. The actual product evaluation process is described in Chap. 21, beginning with a master list of desired and required features, and ending with a formal recommendation by the task force.

Your role in these meetings will be as facilitator, encouraging discussions and compromise. As you will have the most global (if the most superficial) view of what is needed by all the groups, and what is desirable from a technological point of view, you may want to add to the lists generated by the departmental representatives and help identify any irrelevant features that pop up. You may also want to add features that are less important to user groups, such as pricing, installation, training, and support issues.

The group must also determine what weighting scheme to use. For example:

$$0 = \text{Critical}$$
$$1 = \text{Very important}$$
$$2 = \text{Important}$$
$$3 = \text{Desirable but not important}$$

After the group has compiled a master list of all the features, weights will need to be assigned to each, denoting its relative importance. You will have to reconcile differences in opinion on the various weighting suggestions. Majority rule doesn't apply to these discussions. If it is critical to one (and only one) department to have a red-lining feature in the corporate word processor, then it should be incorporated in the list as a critical feature. If a feature is rated as Critical by one department, but only Desirable by all others, it should probably be considered Critical by the task force as a whole.

There may be whole categories of factors that the task force wishes to weight more heavily than other categories. Some examples of these broader groupings include "Ease of Use," "Speed," "Functionality," and "Administrative Issues." If you determine that Functionality is twice as important as Speed, then any score assigned to a product on the basis of its performance on an important "functional" issue will be given twice as much weight as the score received on its performance in a speed test.

An example may help clarify this issue. Perhaps we have determined for our word processor tests that the spell checker feature is very important (an importance rating of 1). We have also created two categories: Speed with a weight of 20, and Functionality with a weight of 40 (Functionality is twice as important to us as Speed). Our tests of the spell checker of each word processor might include a time test (how long does it take to load), as well as a functionality test (does it catch all the misspellings in our test document, and does it come up with appropriate alternatives). The product that scores well in the second test will, all other things being equal, win out over the product that scores well in the speed test.

When testing the various word processors the group will also have to determine the relative importance of each broad category, which will then become an additional multiplier against the features in each category.

The product choice and testing scheme follow the one laid out in Chap. 21. You'll probably want to limit your product list to commercially available products that have a large installed base, if for no other reason than to keep your test base to a manageable number.

Eliminating Noncontenders

Once you have a list of your products, and a list of features, categories, and weights, you will want to begin with the first stage of the research: Eliminating the contenders who do not adhere to the minimal requirements, those features listed as "Critical." While the later stages involve weights and relative scoring, products that do not have even one of the Critical features should be eliminated. This step will eliminate (hopefully) some of your original products, and you may even find that you have to recast your original list to have enough contestants to choose from in later stages. At the end of this stage it will be desirable to have from three to six contenders. You may be able to get away without having to install or even obtain evaluation copies at this early stage, as many of these questions can be answered via vendor calls. In answer to feature availability, when a vendor says "No" that a feature doesn't exist, this information can be relied upon, whereas a "Yes" (particularly when quick and empathic affirmatives follow your every question) should be checked by actual tests.

May the Best Product Prevail

In-depth testing and research begin once the original list has been winnowed down to the semifinalists. These tests include timing tests, user tests, and other manners of qualification. Before beginning the testing phase the task force should develop a test script: What questions will be asked, or tests run to determine a products score, and what results will justify which scores. Perhaps for word processing, spell checking is seen as "Important." Your tests may include the following questions.

1 = Time to load the dictionary

2 = Number of words in the dictionary

3 = Ability to find misspelled words

4 = Legal jargon (your legal department is especially concerned)

The answer to test question 1 will be a stopwatch test result. The answer to test 2 can be found in reference manuals or by calls to the vendor. Test 3 will require a simulated run of the spell checker against a test document. In each case you will develop the test, and then record the tests on the script so that each product uses the same script. If you are using more than one tester, have one tester test the same feature for all products. The learning curve necessary for each tester to become familiar with all the products is higher, but it is the only way to ensure that you are testing the products fairly. It's easy for one tester to come up with radically different results by interpreting the test script differently. As long as the same misinterpretation is made for all products the test results are still comparable. Also, when you have a single person running the tests, that person is better able to see and comment on the variations among products, and to recommend a new test or qualification that will help differentiate the qualities of different products. Back to the word-processing tests, while testing one product the tester may find that one of the spell checkers can manage several user-defined dictionaries. It may be appropriate, if this hasn't been brought up for consideration, to add this to the group of tests for each product.

This example points to the benefits of allowing the tests and feature list to evolve. It will add to the time required to reach a decision, but it will also add to the relative pertinence of the overall tests.

Whenever a vendor is called to confirm a result, record the name, title, and phone number of the person who gave you the information for later reference.

When doing timing tests, do three tests and record the average of the three. It is also better to use automatically timed tests than a stopwatch. Make sure with performance tests that identical platforms are used to get comparable results.

Upon completing the tests, you will have to find a way to normalize all the answers. While some tests may have answers in seconds, some may have yes/no responses, and some another range of answers. The best way to normalize is to establish a scale, perhaps 1 through 4, to place all answers on:

$$4 = \text{Excellent}$$
$$3 = \text{Good}$$
$$2 = \text{Acceptable}$$
$$1 = \text{Poor}$$

For a feature which either exists or not, a yes may be a 3 or 4, and a no may mean 1 or 2. When the range of load times is 0.001 second to 10 seconds, you may determine that anything less than 1 second is a 4 (excellent) while 1–2 seconds is good, 3–7 acceptable, and over 7 is poor. Some of the translation formulas you may be able to ascertain before running the tests; others will be obvious only after the test results are in and you have the relative scale to base the translation on. In some cases, you may opt for a mathematical rule of thumb such as using standard deviations from the mean. In other cases, common sense will be a better guide. In all cases, if you document your reasoning you can defend your choice in the end, or make changes to the formula if objections overrule your initial decision.

Regular meetings should be held during the testing process to update the task force on the progress of tests, and to discuss and integrate new information that has arisen from the testing process. By keeping everyone involved and up to date on the progress, you will minimize the last-minute surprises that come about when members feel they have been left out of the loop.

Implementation

Once an appropriate standard has been agreed to by the group, you need to shift your attention to implementation. There are really three stages to this process. The first is sales. You need to convince all the people affected by this decision that the task force has come up with the right choice, and that in the long run (if not the short run) everyone will benefit. How do you do this? Your task force is in itself a group of disciples who should be bearing the good news to their own departments. They are intimately aware of why this decision is being made, and what the benefits are going to be. Whether progress reports during the evaluation process are called for will vary from situation to situation, but this can be a way to eliminate rumors, confusion, and frustration over the final decision. All users are in this way kept up to date on why the evaluation process is going on and are encouraged to feed information to the task force, through their representative member. There should therefore be no voice left unheard, and no issue left unresolved.

Still the big announcement can unleash a fury of concern, which you will have to be ready to address, and so should be followed closely by a benefits statement, and product demonstrations.

After the "why" you'll have to explain how. How will people transfer from what they were using before to the new standard? How will they be trained? What will happen to the old systems? The best way to address this is on a department-by-department basis. You will find that the needs and concerns will vary from department to department, and while one implementation scheme may work well for one department, it may not be needed in another.

The costs of the implementation will also have to be calculated, and you will want to consider not only the purchase price of the new hardware or software, but the cost of implementation as well.

Finally, you will want to consider when next to review this particular standard. The timing will depend on the technology and how radically and frequently you expect it to change, along with your organization's degree of need to remain on the edge of what's new. It should be reviewed in less than 10 years, and not more than once every 2 years. One reasonable plan would be to meet annually to discuss upgrades to the existing standard, and the need to review the standard as a whole.

Hardware and software will usually maintain an upgrade path that is incrementally more functional, at a fraction of the purchase price. If you have decided to standardize on Microsoft Word as your word processor, you will also standardize on the version that was tested. Different versions of the same product can be just as complicated as different products. On an annual basis the task force reconvenes to determine whether an upgrade is warranted. If the improvements justify the cost of the upgrade, then the transition is made in all cases. Organizations are less and less likely to upgrade each time a new revision is released, as the cost of even a minor upgrade can be significant when the concomitant costs of implementation are included. On the other hand, getting too far out of revision can be costly when the decision is finally made to upgrade. You'll have to make a case-by-case decision on the basis of manufacturer's policy.

To Do

- Determine which products call for standardization first.
- Perform justification analysis.
- Present recommendation to management and get approval.
- Convene task force to evaluate products.
- Establish original list of contenders.
- Determine desired and required features.
- Apply minimum requirements and eliminate noncontenders.
- Perform other tests and determine winner.
- Announce the new standard with reasoning and benefits.
- Start preimplementation sales demonstrations.
- Begin departmental implementation and training.

Chapter 23

Focus Studies

Focus studies are a great way to accomplish a specific goal, or to solve a specific problem, quickly and efficiently. The focus study is really just a compact committee, but since the word *committee* tends to imply a more long-term commitment, a name that underscores its tightly defined nature seems called for. There are four phases to every focus study: goal definition, information gathering, evaluation, and implementation or recommendation. These steps should be rigidly held, so as not lapse into committee status. The focus study group has a short but happy life, accomplishing its objective, that of making a recommendation or implementing a solution, and then disbanding.

The focus study group usually springs from a committee, and reports to that committee. There should be a leader of the focus group, and the number of other people involved (if at all) should remain as small as possible to facilitate quick action. Each member should be motivated to accomplish the stated goal of the study.

The Goal Statement

The key to a successful focus study is in the framing of the objective. If you can't describe the purpose of the focus study in a sentence or two, it isn't focused enough. When you attempt to clarify the problem, you may find yourself with several questions or issues. This means that either you haven't identified the central or underlying issue, or you have more than one focus study on your hands.

For example, during an analysis of your help desk questions the Planning Committee notes that the majority of caller problems relate to printers and printing. You determine that a focus study should be conducted to address this issue. What is the goal?

"Purpose: To find out why people are having printing problems." This might be a valid goal statement, but it doesn't fix the problem. It is really more of a question that needs to be answered on the way to solving the problem.

"Purpose: To reduce the number of printer-related support calls." It sounds right but the need is to eliminate the problems. The support calls will drop as a result. This goal could easily result in a solution that doesn't eliminate the problems but merely reduces the number of calls for support.

"Purpose: To reduce the number of printer-related problems that people experience." This is the central issue after all.

By clearly and correctly establishing your primary goal, you minimize the number of tangents that the study group may take and you will be able to keep everyone focused on the same objective.

Information Gathering

Once you have clearly defined the problem, you will have to lay out your plan of action. List the questions that need to be answered, the information that needs to be gathered, in order for the group to assess the various solutions. In the printer focus study, some of the questions might be:

What are the characteristics of the people who are having these problems?

Are there certain types of printers that are causing the trouble?

Are the problems related to hardware or software?

What resolves the problems?

Each member of the team can go away with questions, research, and action items designed to help gather the information that the group will need to make a decision. Clearly define who is to do what, and how and when it is to be delivered to the group. If a focus study report is going to be delivered to the committee, then the results of any investigation need to be delivered in the form of a report. If you want a spreadsheet or a database file, then say so. Then on the date set for the next meeting, all the information should be in and the group should be ready to move to the next phase.

In the printer problem example, someone will probably return with a subset of the phone-support database. This will be used to generate reports on the characteristics of the callers, as well as the printers.

Option Evaluation

You've got all the information you need and some options may be already apparent. Rather than jumping to an obvious solution, take some time as a group to brainstorm on the possible alternatives, which might uncover a less obvious, but superior solution. To return to our information-gathering example:

What are the characteristics of the people who are having these problems? There are no common characteristics other than the fact that anyone having this problem is attached to the network and is printing to a network printer. Problems are much less common on dedicated printers.

Are there certain types of printers that are causing the trouble? Remote network printers cause the problem, but there are no other common characteristics. Dot matrix, laser, and other brands are all equally likely to cause problems.

Are the problems related to hardware or software? They are operating-system related. The remote printer utility unloads spontaneously.

What resolves the problems? Reload.

Is there an obvious solution? Here are some brainstorming ideas:

1. Get everyone a dedicated printer.
2. Put all printers on the server.
3. Investigate other remote network printer management tools.
4. Train everyone on how to reload the remote printer.
5. Get rid of the network.

After all the brainstorming ideas have been put on the table, you can begin to evaluate each solution as a group. In some cases (see option 3), to fully evaluate a possible solution, you may have to loop back to the information-gathering phase, but once you have all the information, then move on to the implementation or recommendation phase. At the completion of the last phase, the focus study group no longer exists.

It's a straightforward process, with these four phases consistently part of each focus study, but it can be used to solve the toughest problems, quickly and efficiently. Three examples of focus study issues and their questions follow:

Examples

1. Determine whether we should bring any of our publishing projects inside. Questions:

   What types of projects are we outsourcing now?
   Will the quality suffer?
   What hardware would be required to do it in house?
   What software would be required to do it in house?
   What personnel resources would be required?
   How much would it cost?
   How much would it save?

   The head of this focus study would probably report to the planning committee.
   If the recommendation is to bring publishing in house, the committee may begin plans to set up an in-house desktop publishing department.

2. Another focus study might address the question "Should we automate our sales force?" Questions that will have to be answered include:

   What problems are we having now?
   Will an automated system help this?
   What will be some of the new problems if we automate?
   What will be some of the other benefits of automating?
   Are there other solutions?
   What are the costs?

   Again this focus study would report to the planning committee.

3. Another study that would come out of the Security Committee might be organized to answer the question: "Could our competitors get our prospect data files?" This question assumes that the data are valuable and that competitors might try. Information-gathering questions:

   Where are they stored?
   How are they protected?
   How could the security be violated?

To Do

- Frame a goal statement.
- Gather information.
- Evaluate the options.

Chapter 24

Strategic Planning

The Year in Review, the Years Ahead

You've been working all year to put your house in order. You've put out some raging fires, and you're excited about some of the new projects that are under way or at least on the drawing board. You're ready to fly into the new year full steam ahead. Or are you? With a full plate of good projects, it might seem silly to waste any time, but a few moments (or more realistically a few days) spent in thoughtful review and planning will pay off more than you realize.

As early in the year as possible, let all your committees know that the Planning Committee needs year-end reports by the beginning of November. These reports should have conclusions and recommendations summarized for Planning Committee review. Then set aside a few days in November, maybe a week. Get the Planning Committee together, away if possible, to remove everyone from the pull of everyday fires. Your goal during this respite is to review what has transpired over the previous year, and to develop a strategic information systems plan that will be implemented over the next 3 to 10 years.

Every aspect of your role and the areas you have touched on should be reviewed. Begin with your mission statement and the action plans you developed last year. Is the mission statement still valid? Have any of the objectives become obsolete? Are there new objectives that have become pertinent? Which goals were accomplished last year? Of the remaining goals, which should remain, and which should be set aside?

Were there valid reasons for the unrealized goals? What new goals should be introduced? Your review of these issues should point the way to where your efforts should be spent in the coming year.

Each committee has submitted a report for review. What strategic implications are to be found here? Review your departmental focus reports. What new objectives spring from these findings? Your strategic plan is not simply a laundry list of projects, but a cohesive plan with long-term goals that determine the direction of information systems efforts for years to come. The strategic plan will be the compass every committee will use to measure the appropriateness of any one project or plan of action. In some cases, the findings of one committee or task force will indicate the need for a change in the overall strategic direction of your company, and this is why you'll need to review the plan annually vis à vis the committee reports and recommendations. In most cases, however, it is the strategic plan that gives us our guidelines.

Develop new action plans that reflect your changing mission and goals. Keep in mind that there is only a finite number of days in the year, and other resources are equally limited. Do your plans jibe with the available resources? Are there staff, budget, and available time? You and your staff should be measured by your ability to meet these goals, and so the assignment of responsibility should not be given or assumed lightly. Your strategic plan can and should span several years, so spread the goals out over a realistic time frame.

Your goal will be to flesh out the following outline:

Sample Strategic Information Systems Plan
Mission statement (as amended)
Objectives
Goals
   Security
   Support
   Performance improvement
Platform implications
   Hardware
   Software
Training implications
Auditing implications
Action plans
   New projects
   New focus studies
Schedule and budgetary considerations
   Years 1–2
   Years 3–5
   Years 6–10

If your mission statement is unchanged, simply reiterate it now. If it has been amended, then reword it and give your reasons for the change. Your mission statement should evolve over time, but the changes should be a conscious decision to adjust the course of your efforts, rather than a random or unplanned reaction to events. Following a mission statement that never changes will lead you astray as surely as one that changes yearly.

Trickle-Down Planning

While your mission gives the broadest definition of your role as systems manager, your objectives state more specifically how that role translates into action. While your mission may refer to your role as the protector of secure and vital data, an objective might be to establish policies and procedures to ensure that every piece of data is secure to the degree prescribed by its nature. This in turn might translate into several goals, one of which might be: to create an inventory of all data and the security and criticality rating of each. This goal will at last be translated into action plans which can be carried out over the course of the year.

There should be goals and action plans to fulfill each of the stated objectives. If your objectives correspond to security, support, and performance issues, then so too should your goals and plans.

There are usually hardware and software implications of these goals and these can be brought together into a cohesive plan for changes in platform standards. This approach will help prevent individual goals from reaching conflicting conclusions with respect to hardware or software, and resulting in unwise purchasing decisions. This one area has the potential for causing the most contention among the group, because the choices are often exclusive—one alternative precluding another—and because personal preferences are hard to eliminate. If the goals and objectives are clearly stated, and put into a priority order, then the right choice may be more evident, but more often there will be two or three firmly entrenched camps, between which you'll have to negotiate.

When the goals are translated into action plans, we see specifically what needs to happen. This translation process is more appropriately done at the individual committee level, so that the goals all need to be distributed back to the committees, which will in turn translate the goals into action plans.

Action Plans

Regardless of who writes the action plans, these critical components must be carefully written if they are to correctly perform their function.

First, they must state which goal and objective they will help to obtain. This ties the action plan back to the mission statement so that you don't have projects without purpose.

Second, they should state measurable outcomes, or deliverables, that will be forthcoming. It might be a document, the implementation of a new standard, or the completion of a training course. By stating the desired outcome, you will be able to say conclusively at the end of the year whether or not the plan was carried out. Some deliverables will also indicate the achievement of a specific goal, while others are steps along the way to a longer-range goal.

Identify the responsible parties: who does what, and when. Specific tasks are more desirable than general responsibilities, and specific dates are better than vague time frames. These dates should be reflective of the other responsibilities and scheduled activities that will be undertaken by the people involved. Realistic schedules should be conservative, since schedules tend to slip more often than they gain slack.

Budgetary implications should also be included. Don't forget to include time in the form of hours or days devoted to a task, since it may be the single most costly factor involved and can easily be overlooked when no outlay of cash is involved.

Budget and Schedule

The individual action plan schedules and budgets can be used to extrapolate forward and come up with schedules and budgets for the overall strategic plan. The plan can and should span more than 1 year, with 3-, 5- and 10-year planning horizons being the most common. The larger the goal, and the broader the implications, the farther the horizon will be pushed. If, for instance, you will be converting all your workstations to a new operating system, and your custom programs to a new language, the horizon may realistically be 5 to 10 years. Since the plan discusses more distant goals, the specific action plans and budgets will be more vague and the dates for accomplishment may be more realistically set as a range rather than a specific date.

Improvement Plans

During your Planning Committee discussions, and over the course of the year, you'll see several areas where there is room for improvement. There's always room for improvement.

While the strategic plan discusses new projects to help obtain specific goals, you are also interested in doing whatever it is you're currently doing better. If there is no time for strategic planning, no resources for new projects, then there is all the more reason for improvement planning, because with such limited resources you need to make headway wherever you can.

Suggestions may come from voluntary feedback in the form of a suggestion box, from interviews, by chance, through observation, or from technological breakthroughs. Gather them in, write them down, along with their costs and the department which will most benefit, and then juggle them into a list ordered by priority, and balanced by an even distribution from department to department.

The budget for computer improvements may be influenced by this list. If you have a realistic sense of what can be spent, and a demonstrable rationale for why it should be spent on the top 10 items on your improvement list, you may get what you ask for. On the other hand, you may be handed a figure (always less than what it will take to implement everything on your list) and you'll have to determine how best to create the biggest bang for this buck.

What workstations need to be upgraded for faster performance, fewer support calls, and less expensive maintenance costs? Look at the software. Will the right tool for the job make a big difference? Who's wasting the most time on manual or misused applications? Will training a group of users add to their productivity and make overall gains in the efficiency of various systems?

Is this plan achievable within the budget cycle? Are there other requirements that will drive the actual cost of this project up? Who will have the responsibility for this project, and can they manage the time requirements? What are the long-term ramifications?

Managers may stipulate the format of your proposed improvement plan, with the points they wish to consider. If you are not guided otherwise, here is an outline that will cover all the necessary points in a way that gives answers immediately and backs them up with detail when and if that's necessary.

Microcomputer Systems Improvement Plan for 199X
Executive Summary Background
    Why this plan is being presented
    Objectives
    Scope
Summary of Recommendations
    For each recommendation in order of importance:
        Actions
        Benefits
        Requirements
        Costs

    Measurable outcomes
    Milestones
    Implementation schedule
    Responsibilities
    Implications
    Suggested budget and schedule
    Backup data

  Management can use this format to make final decisions on the basis of an a priori budget. Ask the decision-making group to look down your list of recommendations and check off each one that it feels has benefits that justify the cost and draw a red line below the item where the money runs out. If you make group members' jobs easier, they'll be grateful, and you'll accomplish more of what you want.

  The executive summary should be a one-page synopsis of the contents of your proposal. Try to sum up each section in a sentence and stress the bottom-line issues.

  Your background section should orient the reader. This is often hard to do, simply because it appears so obvious. To get the right reference point, imagine that a new person had to step in for your boss, and this report had to be sent to this person in your absence. You'll want to explain why you are providing this report, what its objectives are, and what it covers in scope.

  In your summary of recommendations, you will want to list each plan based on its order of importance.

  For each recommendation you will want to include not only a description of the purchase or project, but the key benefits that will be derived from the effort. If, for instance, you want to upgrade all 286 machines to 425SX machines with 4 Mbytes RAM, you will want to list the benefits that this upgrade will bring in terms of speed and the ability to run more current applications. Include both quantifiable and soft benefits when appropriate.

  You will also have to include cost figures. Try to identify all the cost implications, even if you're not sure of the exact amounts. Nothing has the potential to upset management quite like unexpected costs, particularly if it looks as though there was any kind of cover-up during the planning process. If you get the reputation for springing these unpleasant surprises, future expenditures will have a tougher time getting approved.

  Cost of time for in-house staff has to be considered. If there are internal hourly cost figures, you can use these. These numbers may seem to overly inflate the perceived cost of a project and you may be tempted to forgo them. After all, since you're there anyway, why treat it as an additional cost? But when you consider the cost of introducing a new technology, and if the training time for each person to learn it is 4 hours, the overall cost to the organization in terms of lost time is substantial, so where do you draw the line? One way around separating this cost from other more direct dollar outlays is to include it in its own subheading under "time." This exculpates you from not including the cost, but doesn't confuse it with other, more hard dollars.

If there are prerequisites to achieving the goals of this project, they should be itemized. If it isn't obvious why a particular requirement is necessary, explain it. These are often the individual cost factors.

Whenever possible list the measurable outcomes from the project. The measurable outcome is a tangible indicator of the completion of the project—the project's deliverable result.

Milestones are used as intermediate markers of accomplishment, and they also serve to help management visualize how the project will progress. The implementation schedule will often be tied to milestones, showing what will happen when. Responsibilities assign specific people or outside organizations with the tasks at hand. Implications is an area where any other discussions can take place regarding spin-off topics that should be noted.

The difference between the strategic plan and the improvement plan is blurred, and what may suffice as an improvement plan in a small company may come under the purview of a strategic plan of a larger organization. One difference seems to be that the strategic plan is more forward-looking, and has a tendency to define budget and staffing implications, while the improvement plan is carried out more in the short term, and in recognition of a specific budget amount.

The following plan for the replacement of the top five systems with state-of-the-art processors is more typical of an improvement plan recommendation, while the second plan—the implementation of an E-mail system, is more indicative of a strategic plan:

Plan: Upgrade the five high-end processors
Benefits:
    Speed up most time-consuming processes by up to 50 percent
    Redistributing hardware down the line, upgrading the processing time of all systems
    Getting engineers familiar with state-of-the-art equipment for competitive advantage
    Viewed as a perk to engineering staff
Costs:
    High-end workstation cost—$3500 each
    Installation and setup—$500 each

Installation of transferred machines—$500 each
Support follow-up—$2000
Milestones and schedule:
Purchase machines—day 1
Installation and setup—day 5–day 10
Transfer machines—day 10–day 30
Responsibilities:
Install hardware and software: Greg Almath
Support: In-house support team
Implications:
None

Plan: To set up e-mail among all administration
Benefits:
Elimination of telephone tag
Immediate access to messages
Immediate receipt of interstate mail
Reduced paper flow
Ease of distribution to groups
Easy filing for archival and retrieval systems
Costs:
E-mail server—$3000
E-mail package with license—$150–$5000
Installation and setup—$500
Training—$7500
Support—$5000
Milestones and schedule:
E-mail up and running—day 1–day 30
Training—day 30–day 60
Complete—day 60
Responsibilities:
Install hardware and software: E-mail Magic, Meriden
Training: Able Training Group, West Falls
Support: Tuned-in Support, Granby
Implications:
Only those staff members who currently have workstations on their desks will be set up with a mail box. Over the next 3 years we expect all staff to have computer access from their desk.

As you write your own plans, you will find that some work well with these headings and some don't. Rather than sticking to any one format rigidly, use those that make sense and cast off the ones that don't. The headings included here are should-considers rather than must-includes. The only three that must be in every plan are the description, the benefits, and the costs.

To Do

- Send out notice to all committees requiring year-end report by October 31.
- Schedule retreat for Planning Committee in November.
- Determine outline for the strategic plan.
- Get budget for improvement plan for coming year.

Appendix A

PC Management Tools

The following list will help you to get a hold of the tools needed to do your job. At the beginning of each section is a brief description of the product category. A list of features follows. The products list will give you the names of products and their manufacturer.

Backup utilities

Description

Performs backup and archival functions for LAN systems, and assists in the management of backup media.

Features

Automated, unattended backup at off times

Server-based backup

Ability to backup local hard-drives and remote servers

Data compression and encryption

Virus protection

File viewing

Log reports to help find files for restore

Backup labeling

Device management to monitor backup hardware problems

Drive chaining to handle multiple backup sessions on one tape

Disk mirroring of server volumes, directories or files

Ability to backup open files

Products

ARCserve, Cheyenne

Central Point Backup, Central Point Software Inc.

LANshadow, Horizons Technology, Inc.

Palindrome Backup Director, Palindrome Corporation

Palindrome HSM Software, Palindrome Corporation

Palindrome Network Archivist, Palindrome Corporation

Palindrome Prepare!, Palindrome Corporation

Disk file management/diagnostic/recovery tools

Description

Assists in the management and organization of disk files, as well as the recovery of damaged files from disk media.

Features

File compression

File viewing

Repairs common disk problems

Diagnostics to identify potential hardware problems

Optimizers to defragment disks

Products

CheckIt Pro, Touchstone Software Corporation

XTree, Central Point Software Inc.

PC Tools, Central Point Software Inc.

Norton Commander, Symantec Corporation

Ontrack Data Recovery, Ontrack

FAX/MODEM communication tools

Description

Supports the use of facsimiles and modems in a LAN environment.

Features

Fax and receive directly from workstations

Inbound routing of faxes to other users

Hardware independence

MHS e-mail compliance

Activity Log to record network communication activity

Direct connection to mini and mainframe computers

Limit access to modems by node address

Modem/Fax groups definable

Multiple parties able to view communication over a single line

Monitor connection and communication traffic

Name modems and faxes

Reset modems/faxes without rebooting server

Set automatic timeouts for improperly released connections

Access over bridged networks and routers

Products

FAXserver, Cheyenne

NET SatisFAXtion, Intel

WinFax PRO, Delrina

Helpdesk tools

Description

Assistance in logging, routing, troubleshooting, and responding to helpdesk calls.

Features

Call Handling

Sorting of call information in various ways for easy retrieval

Keyword searching

Response support including dialing assistance, letter/fax generation and batch mailing assistance

Time tracking, stopwatch function

Help with diagnosis

User information storage to track installed products, configuration, and call history

Defect tracking

Flexible query and reporting capabilities

Interface with inventory applications

Products

Customer Response System (CRS), Syspro Corporation

Customer Service Management System (CSM), Clarify Inc.

Support Express, Software Marketing Group, Inc.

Vantive Helpdesk, The Vantive Corporation

Vantive Quality, The Vantive Corporation

Vantive Support, The Vantive Corporation

Network management utilities

Description

Assistance in the overall management of the LAN, including control, monitoring, diagnosing, auditing, and reporting.

Features

Collect and store configuration data on workstations

Centralized storage of configuration data

Graphical monitoring of resource usage

Filter information to limit the scope of reports

Detect and notify when new components are added

Reporting that includes sorting, grouping, subtotals, and suppressing duplicate fields

Scheduling jobs for later execution

Recommends corrective action

History reports

Statistics on resources, current and historic

Set alarm thresholds

Set to run in background

Ability to monitor individual workstations

Packet capture for in-depth diagnostic investigation

Ability to disable ports remotely

Event manager

To do list

Workstation desktop control

Diskspace monitoring

Run jobs across multiple servers

Statistics including totals, minimum, maximum, and average values

Audits of station lockouts

Reports of file server time changes

Disk space analysis

User documentation including SysCon info, trustee assignments

File server documentation

Information on printer and queue configurations

Assistance with software version control

Select critical resource alarms to alert you to potential problems

Notification of problems sent through e-mail, fax, or pager

Ability to set baselines and determine changes from baseline

Ability to calculate available addresses

Ability to create management domains of various servers

Internet and other connectivity testing and viewing

Detailed information on installed hardware, software

Reporting on various network performance statistics

Ability to import and export data

Topology independence

Products

Bindview, LAN Support Group

Brightwork Fusion, McAfee Associates

LANalyzer, Novell

LAN Automatic Inventory, McAfee Associates

LAN Directory, Frye Computer Systems, Inc.

LANauditor, Horizons Technology, Inc.

LANDesk Manager, Intel

LANlord, Central Point Software Inc.

MicroKit, Micropath

MicroTrack, Micropath

Monitrix, Cheyenne

NetControl, Central Point Software Inc.

NetSight Sentry, Intel

NetWare Management Agent, Novell

NetWare Manager, Frye Computer Systems, Inc.

Node Tracker, Frye Computer Systems, Inc.

Node Vision, Fresh NetSoft Inc.

Norton Administrator, Symantec Corporation

Origen, Preferred Systems, Inc.

Saber LAN Workstation, Saber Software Corporation

Visinet, VisiSoft

Power management and diagnostic tools

Description

Monitors power fluctuations that may present a danger to your systems and take the necessary measures to protect systems.

Features

Shuts down your system safely

Notifies users of shutdown due to power loss

Tests your UPS and reports to you periodically

Graphic displays of UPS status

Power event log

Automatic notification of problems to remote locations via paging or e-mail technology

Scheduled system shutdown and reboot

Monitors the power disturbances and quality

Set alarms to notify you of potentially dangerous situations

Automatic rebooting

Multiple server monitoring

Products

Minuteman Lanmaster, Para Systems, Inc.

Power Alert Plus, Tripp Lite

PowerChute, American Power Conversion

Printer management tools

Description

Assistance in the management of shared printing resources on a LAN.

Features

Speed up printing

Installed on workstations or server

Notify print job owner of changes in printer status

Support several print queues

Logs print jobs to file

Ability to view, and control print jobs

Server and workstation based options

Ability to change order, copies, queues, and other factors

Products

LaserPrinter Assist, Fresh NetSoft, Inc.

NetportExpress, Intel

LanspoolExpress, Intel

Printer Assist, Fresh NetSoft, Inc.

PS-Print/QueueIT!, McAfee Associates

Q Assist, Fresh NetSoft, Inc.

Remote access

Description

Assistance in the management and control of remote users, and remote access to workstations for assistance and training purposes.

Features

Ability to operate one or more remote stations

Scan for available workstation

Ability to reboot with automatic reconnect

Setup remote tasks to logon to remote station and run programs

Security to lockout or alert on takeover

Password control

Remote site keyboard and mouse suppression

Remote diagnostics

File transfer capabilities

Ability to establish IPX connection

Automated dial-back security

Event logging

Data compression

Modem pooling

Connections between LANs

Chat feature to allow communication between master and remote

Display remote configuration information

Allow access without taking over, look only

Products

Carbon Copy, Microcom, Inc.

Close-Up, Norton-Lambert Corporation

LAN Assist, Microtest

MAP Assist, Microtest

MicroAnnex NCS, Xylogics, Inc.

NETremote +

Norton pcANYWHERE, Symantec Corporation

Proxy, Funk Software, Inc.

RemoteExpress, Intel

WanderLink, Funk Software, Inc.

Security systems

Description

Enhancing the safety and protective measures in a LAN environment.

Features

Audits all user activity including program execution and various types of file access

Show changes to users on network

Show trustee and user information

Security equivalencies

Monitor uploads from floppy to network

File locking

File encryption

Prevent floppy boots

Guest access with limited rights

Disallow interruption of boot process

Report on login and logout times

Password management

Monitor users over multiple servers

Remotely configure and distribute security

Track modifications made to the bindery

Flexible query and reporting capabilities

Single sign-on

Products

AuditWare, Preferred Systems, Inc.

Bindview, LAN Support Group

Brightwork Fusion, McAfee Associates

LANtrail, Horizons Technology, Inc.

Norton DiskLock, Symantec Corporation

PC/DACS, Mergent International, Inc.

Site/DACS, Mergent International, Inc.

Software distribution

Description

Automatic distribution of software and other updates to remote workstations and servers.

Features

Automate new server installs

Preconfigure systems

Clone user or server information

Modification and delivery of rights, queues, login scripts

Reports and query options

Group distribution lists

Delivery across Multiple servers

Undo capabilities

New installations and upgrade management

Password synchronization

Products

NetWare Navigator, Novell

Norton Administrator, Symantec Corporation

Origen, Preferred Systems, Inc.

SUDS, Frye Computer Systems, Inc.

Software metering tools

Description

Managing the licensing process to ensure that neither too few or too many people are using software copies.

Features

Ability to limit usage beyond licensed amount

Provide exception reports to show when excess copies are in use

Virus protection built in

Flexible rules for access

Ability to borrow copies from other servers

Graphic display of current usage

Ability to export files

Define authorization to certain applications

Identify VIPs who will always have access to all applications

Reports on historical data

Notifies users when an application is available for use

Products

AppMeter, Funk Software, Inc.

Norton Administrator, Symantec Corporation

SiteMeter, McAfee Associates

Saber LAN Workstation, Saber Software Corporation

Saber Enterprise Application Manager, Saber Software Corporation

Software Metering and Resource Tracking (SMART), Frye Computer Systems, Inc.

Workload management

Description

Assistance in managing resource for load-balancing and resource sharing objectives.

Features

Ability to handle heavy jobs at off-peak times

Offload work to specific task server

Event manager

Notification of task status

Queue management capabilities

Allow for tasks to be submitted regularly

Support multiple queues

Log file to record activity

Flexible query and reporting functions

Products

NetWare Console Commander, Frye Computer Systems, Inc.

OnQueue, NetPlus Software, Inc.

Origen, Preferred Systems, Inc.

Saber LAN Workstation, Saber Software Corporation

Virus protection

Description
To protect against virus infection.

Features
Software will disallow logins without virus protecting in place

Automatic distribution of updates from server to workstations

Alerts via e-mail, fax, paging systems at time of detection

Software will take predetermined action upon receiving a threat

Continuous scanning of file activity

Virus monitoring and alarms to alert you to possible infections

Protection against entry and propagation of viruses into the server and throughout the LAN

Removal of viruses including unknown, polymorphic (self-modifying) and stealth (self-concealing) viruses

Protection of compressed files

Protection of multiple workstation operating systems

Products
Central Point Anti-Virus, Central Point Software Inc.

Dr Solomon's Anti-Virus Toolkit, Ontrack

InocuLAN, Cheyenne

Norton AntiVirus, Symantec Corporation

Appendix B

Manufacturer and Product List

American Power Conversion
132 Fairgrounds Road
West Kingston, RI 02892
(401) 789-5735

    PowerChute, Power Management and Diagnostic Tools

Central Point
15220 NW GreenBrier Parkway
Suite 150
Beaverton, OR 97006
(800) 876-6368

    PC Tools, Disk File Management/Diagnostic/Recovery Tools
    XTree, Disk File Management/Diagnostic/Recovery Tools
    NetControl, Network Management Utilities
    LANlord, Inventory Tools
    Central Point Anti-Virus, Virus Protection
    Central Point Backup, Backup Utilities

Cheyenne
3 Expressway Plaza
Roslyn Heights, NY 11577
(800) 243-9462

    ARCserve, Backup Utilities
    FAXserve, FAX/MODEM Communication Tools

InocuLAN, Virus Protection

Monitrix, Inventory Tools, Network Management Utilities

Clarify Inc.
2702 Orchard Parkway
San Jose, CA 95134
(408) 428-2000

Customer Service Management System (CSM), Helpdesk Tools

Delrina Corporation
895 Don Mills Road
#2 Park Center
Suite 500
Don Mills, Ontario M3C 1W3

WinFax PRO, FAX/MODEM Communication Tools

Fresh NetSoft, Inc.
1819 E. Southern Ave.
Suite A10
Mesa, AZ 85204
(602) 497-4628

Node Vision, Network Management Utilities

Printer Assist, Printer Management Tools

Laser Assist, Printer Management Tools

Q Assist, Printer Management Tools

Frye Computer Systems, Inc.
19 Temple Place
Boston, MA 02111
(617) 451-5400

NetWare Early Warning System, Network Management Utilities

NetWare Console Commander, Workload Management

Node Tracker, Network Management Utilities

LAN Directory, Network Management Utilities

SUDS, Software Distribution

Software Metering and Resource Tracking (SMART), Software Metering Tools

Funk Software, Inc.
222 Third Street
Cambridge, MA 02142
(617) 497-6339

    AppMeter, Software Metering Tools

    Proxy, Remote Access

    WanderLink, Remote Access

Horizons Technology, Inc.
3990 Ruffin Road
San Diego, CA 92123
(619) 292-8331

    LANauditor, Network Management Utilities

    LANshadow, Backup Utilities

    LANtrail, Security Systems

Intel Corp
5200 NE Elam Young Parkway
Hillsboro, OR 90124
(800) 538-3373

LANDesk Manager, Network Management Utilities

    LanspoolExpress, Printer Management Tools

    NetSight Sentry, Network Management Utilities

    RemoteExpress, Remote Access

    NET SatisFAXtion, FAX/MODEM Communication Tools

    NetportExpress, Printer Management Tools

LAN Support Group
2425 Fountainview
Suite 390
Houston, TX 77057
(800) 749-8439

    Bindview, Network Management Utilities

McAfee Associates/Brightwork Development Corp
766 Shrewsbury Ave.
Jerral Center West
Tinton Falls, NJ 07724
(908) 530-0440

    Brightwork Fusion, Network Management Utilities, Software Metering Tools

    SiteMeter, Software Metering Tools

    LAN Automatic Inventory

    NETremote+, Remote Access

    PS-Print/QueueIT!, Printer Management Tools

Mergent International, Inc.
70 Inwood Road
Rocky Hill, CT 06067
(203) 257-4223

    PC/DACS, Security Systems

    Site/DACS, Security Systems

Microcom, Inc.
500 River Ridge Drive
Norwood, MA 02062
(617) 551-1000

    Carbon Copy, Remote Access

Micropath
10900 Northeast Eighth Street
Suite 900
Bellevue, WA 98004
(206) 454-2676

    MicroKit, Network Management Utilities

    MicroTrack, Network Management Utilities

Microtest
4747 N. 22nd Street
Phoenix, AZ 85016-4700
(602) 952-6400

LAN Assist, Remote Access

MapAssist, Remote Access

Norton-Lambert Corporation
PO Box 4085
Santa Barbara, CA 93140
(805) 964-6767

Close-Up, Remote Access

Ontrack
6321 Bury Drive
Suite 15-19
Eden Prairie, MN 55346
(800) 872-2599

Ontrack Data Recovery, Disk File Management/Diagnostic/Recovery Tools

Dr Solomon's Anti-Virus Toolkit, Virus Protection

Para Systems, Inc.
1455 LeMay Drive
Carrollton, TX 75007
(800) 238-7272

Minuteman Lanmaster, Power Management and Diagnostic Tools

NetPlus Software, Inc.
47 Wake Robin Road
Sudbury, MA 01776
(508) 443-6043

OnQueue, Workload Management

Novell, Inc.
122 E. 1700 S.
Provo, UT 84606
(801) 429-7000

LANalyzer, Network Management Utilities

NetWare Navigator, Software Distribution

NetWare Management Agent, Network Management Utilities

Palindrome Corporation
600 East Diehl Road
Naperville, IL 60563
(708) 505-3300

    Palindrome Backup Director, Backup Utilities

    Palindrome HSM Software, Backup Utilities

    Palindrome Network Archivist, Backup Utilities

    Palindrome Prepare!, Backup Utilities

Preferred Systems, Inc.
250 Captain Thomas Blvd.
West Haven, CT 06516
(800) 222-7638

    Origen, Network Management Utilities, Software Distribution, Workload Management

    AuditWare, Security Systems

Saber Software Corporation
5944 Luther Lane
Suite 1007
Dallas, TX 75225
(800) 338-8754

    Saber LAN Workstation, Network Management Utilities, Software Metering Tools, Workload Management

    Saber Enterprise Application Manager, Software Metering Tools

Software Marketing Group, Inc.
108 3rd Street
Des Moines, IA 50309
(800) 395-0209

    Support Express, Helpdesk Tools

Symantec Corporation
10201 Torre Ave.
Cupertino, CA 95014
(408) 253-9600

    Norton Administrator, Network Management Utilities, Software Distribution, Software Metering Tools

Norton AntiVirus, Virus Protection

Norton Commander, Disk File Management/Diagnostic/Recovery Tools

Norton DiskLock, Security Systems

Norton pcANYWHERE, Remote Access

Synergy Solutions Inc.
2150 South Country Club, Suite 1
Mesa, AZ 85210
(602) 545-9797

Modem Assist Plus, FAX/MODEM Communication Tools

Syspro Corporation
P.O. Box 243
Orinda, CA 94563
(510) 254-9755

Customer Response System (CRS), Helpdesk Tools

Touchstone Software Corporation
2130 Main Street
Suite 250
Huntington Beach, CA 92648
(714) 969-7746

CheckIt Pro, Disk File Management/Diagnostic/Recovery Tools

Tripp Lite
500 N. Orleans
Chicago, IL 60610
(312) 329-1777

Power Alert Plus, Power Management and Diagnostic Tools

The Vantive Corporation
1100 Abernathy Road
Suite 1720
Atlanta, GA 30328
(800) 582-6848

Vantive Support, Helpdesk Tools

Vantive Quality, Helpdesk Tools

Vantive Helpdesk, Helpdesk Tools

VisiSoft
2700 NE Expressway
Suite B700
Atlanta, GA 30345
(404) 320-0077

Visinet, Network Management Utilities

Xylogics, Inc.
53 Third Ave.
Burlington, MA 01803
(800) 889-9229

MicroAnnex NCS, Remote Access

Bibliography

Books

Bates, Regis J. Jr., *Disaster Recover Planning,* McGraw-Hill, New York, 1992.
Davis, Peter T., *Complete LAN Security and Control,* Windcrest/McGraw-Hill, New York, 1994.
Fox, Jackie, and Martin Waterhouse, *Introduction to Hard Disk Management,* Que Corporation, Carmel, Ind., 1992.
Madron, Thomas W., *Network Security in the 90's.* John Wiley & Sons, New York, 1992.
Mayo, Johnathan L., *Computer Viruses,* Windcrest, Blue Ridge Summit, PA, 1989.
Nimmer, Raymond T., *The Law of Computer Technology,* Warren Gorham Lamont, Boston, 1992.
Russell, Deborah, and G. T. Gangemi Sr., *Computer Security Basics,* O'Reilly & Associates, Sebastopol, Calif., 1991.
Seymour, Jim, *Jim Seymour's PC Productivity Bible,* Brady Books-Simon and Schuster, New York, 1991.
Wilson, Art, *Help! The Art of Computer Technical Support,* Peachpit Press, Berkeley, 1991.

Periodicals

Berline, Gary, and Catherine Kunkemueller, "Power Protectors: Surge Suppressors Clamp Down on Spikes," *PC Magazine,* vol. 11(16):335–358, Sept. 29, 1992.
Ellison, Carol, "On Guard: 20 Utilities That Battle the Virus Threat," *PC Magazine,* vol. 10(18):199–280, Oct. 29, 1991.
Musthaler, Linda P., and Brian R. Musthaler, "Diaster Recovery Planning," *Stacks: The Network Journal,* vol. 1(1):29–33, May 1993.
Olympia, P. L., "LAN Data Security," *DMBS,* vol. 5(9):97–99, August 1992.
Reed, Suzanne, "The LAN Security Nightmare," *Reseller Management,* vol. 16(1):44–48, Jan. 1993.
St. Clair, Melanie, "Beyond Batteries," *LAN Magazine,* vol. 7(11):137–145, Nov. 1992.
Stang, David J., "Virus Dangers to NetWare LANs," *NetWare Connection,* pp. 10–22, Jan./Feb. 1993.
Zanger, Larry, "The legal risks involved in copying PC software," *The Network Report,* vol. 7(7):20–32, July 1992.

Index

Academic background of systems managers, 6
Access audits, 109–116
   motives for unauthorized access and, 109–111
   solutions to unauthorized access and, 111–113
   standard security precautions and, 115–116
   systems security analysis and, 113–115
Accessibility:
   criticality analysis and, 63
   unauthorized access and, 106–107
   (*See also* Access audits)
Action plans, 21–22
   organizing and, 27
   strategic planning and, 235–236
Addition of new applications (*see* Application additions or revisions)
Administrative screen for help desk, 141
Advertising for systems managers, 2–3
Antiviral programs, 96, 97, 254
Application additions or revisions:
   backup process and, 84, 86
   getting notification of, 54, 84, 86
   request form for, 129
Application audit form, 126, 127
Application form for systems managers, 3–6
Application inventory form, 57, 58
Application revision request form, 129
Applications:
   additions or revisions of (*see* Application additions or revisions)
   custom (*see* Custom software)
   database (*see* Databases)
   document management and (*see* Document management)
   inventory of, 57–58
   spreadsheet (*see* Spreadsheets)
   systems managers' experience with, 8
Archives, 183–184
Area experts, 42
Attitudes for help desk, 137–140

Audits:
   access (*see* Access audits)
   backup (*see* Backup audits)
   of database systems, 188–189
   for disaster plan, 71–72
   of hard disk (*see* Disk audits)
   legal (*see* Legal audits)
   of source code (*see* Source code audits)
AUTOEXEC.BAT file, 174
Automated project managers, 31

Backup audits, 77–92
   damaged areas on disk and, 88
   data corruption and, 88–89
   datapath failure and, 89
   deleted files and, 87
   file types and, 78–79
   forewarning users of, 91
   frequency and methods for, 81–84
   full disk recovery and, 89–92
   logs and tools for, 79–81
   media failure and, 89
   reasons for, 77–78
   restoration process and, 84–87
   results of, 91–92
   testing level of protection and, 86–89
Backup log, 31, 32, 80
Backup procedures audit form, 90
Backup utilities, 243–244
Backups:
   compliance with procedures for, 79–80
   criticality analysis and, 65–66
   of custom software, 128–129
   frequency of, 70
   of hard drives, 81
   labeling, 81–84, 89
   media for, 80–81
   off-site, 70–71
   offsite, 112–113
   policies and procedures for, 65–66, 77–78
   before preventive maintenance, 117
   protecting against viruses, 96–97
   software for, 80
   viruses and, 93
   (*See also* Backup audits)

Barriers to learning, overcoming, 148–149
Batteries, replacing, 120
Blackouts, protection against, 121, 122
Brainstorming:
　about new technologies, 215
　focus studies and, 229
Brownouts, protection against, 121, 122
Budgets, strategic planning and, 236
Business disaster plan, 68–70

Cables, reseating, 119–120
Calendar section of Master Planner binder, 27–28
Call support form, 142
Can-do approach for help desk, 137–138
Cards, reseating, 119–120
Challenge as reason for accessing files without authorization, 110
Chaos theory, 179–180
Classified ads for systems managers, 2–3
Classroom training, 149
Client support:
　as objective, 19
　(See also Help desk)
Clients, legal responsibility for viral contamination of disks shipped to, 105
Coaching:
　to encourage spreadsheet use, 186
　as training method, 150
Commercial software:
　access to, 56
　corporate policy for use of, 100–101
　inventory of, 55–57
　licenses of (see Licenses of commercial software)
　modified, 130–131
　unauthorized (see Legal audit; Piracy)
Commercial software inventory form, 56
Committees, 35–42
　chair of, 36
　etiquette for, 35–38
　goals of, 41–42
　leading, 36–37
　length of meetings for, 37
　membership of, 36
　Planning, 39–42

Committees (*Cont.*):
　reason for meeting of, 35–36
　recordkeeping and, 37
　schedule of meetings for, 40–42
　Security
　　(*See also* Criticality analysis; Disaster planning; specific committees and subcommittees)
Communication, newsletters for (*see* Newsletters)
Communication skills for systems managers, 6
Communications focus, 201–205
　communications map and, 201–203
　departmental recommendations and, 205
　ladder of communication and, 203
　new technologies for, 204–205
　wide area direct connection advantages and, 203–204
Communications map, 201–203
Communications subcommittee, 39–40
　(*See also* Communications focus)
Compliance with backup procedures, 79–80
Contact lists for disaster plan, 71
Contracts:
　for custom software rights, 104
　with outside vendors, 105–106
Copyright violations, 99–101
CPU inventory form, 49–50, 52
Crashes, restoration process and, 89
Criteria for new technologies, 216–217
Criticality analysis sheet, 65
Criticality ratings, 61–66
　accessibility and, 63
　backup policies and procedures and, 65–66
　backup requirements and, 78–79
　disaster plan and, 70
　integrity and, 64
　Security Committee and, 62–63
　sensitivity and, 64
　source code audits and, 127
　strategic links and, 64–65
　systems list for, 62
　virus protection and, 97
Curiosity as reason for accessing files without authorization, 109–110
Custom applications, source code audits and (*see* Source code audits)

Custom software:
  backups of, 79, 128–129
  development tools and documentation of, 127–128
  input/output and testing methods for, 128
  locating, 125–127
  protection of source code and, 79
  revision management for, 129–130
  rights to, 104–106

Data:
  desensitization of, 112
  insurance coverage for, 72, 73
  protection of, Security Committee and, 38–39
  separating in subdirectories, 170
  taken off premises, security of, 112–113
  volatile, backup protection of, 78–79
Data compression techniques, 172–173
Data corruption, restoration process and, 88–89
Data loss form, 84, 85
Databases, 187–189
  auditing, 188–189
  for departmental focus study, 197
  encouraging use of, 187–188
  for keeping track of inventory, 54
  systems managers' experience with, 7
  tracking applications and, 188
Datapath failure, restoration process and, 89
Demonstrations, 149–150
Departmental focus study, 191–199
  follow-up of, 198
  initial meeting for, 192
  results and recommendations of, 197–198
  time study analysis and, 192–197
Departmental focus study overview form, 193–194
Desensitization of sensitive data, 112
Diagnostics, 174
Dial-up lines, 204
Dialback software to prevent unauthorized access to files, 111–112
Direct lines, 204
Directories, standardizing, 170
Disaster planning, 67–73
  audit procedures and, 71–72
  business disaster plan and, 68–70

Disaster planning (*Cont.*):
  criticality ratings and, 70
  insurance coverage and, 72–73
  isolating critical components and, 67–68
  off-site backups and, 70–71
  responding to disasters and, 71
Disaster planning subcommittee, 38
Disk analyzers, 172
Disk audits, 171–177
  external review and, 173–174
  internal checks and, 172–173
  organization of drive and, 174
  performance-tuning tools and, 174, 176
Disk diagnostics, 120
Disk file management diagnostic/recovery tools, 244
Disk space:
  checking, 173
  use by large spreadsheets, 187
Disks:
  damaged areas on, restoration process and, 88
  floppy (*see* Floppy disks)
  full disk recovery and, 89–92
  hard (*see* Disk audits; Hard-disk maintenance; Hard drives)
  hardware maintenance and, 120
  (*See also* Drives)
Displaced workers, new technologies and, 217–218
Document analysis form, 181
Document management, 179–184
  chaos theory of, 179–180
  document analysis and, 180–182
  document-sharing requirements and, 181–182
  options for, 183–184
Drills for disaster plan, 71–72
Drive types, standardizing on, 169
Drives:
  floppy, cleaning heads of, 120
  hard (*see* Disk audits; Hard-disk maintenance; Hard drives)
  parking, 173
  (*See also* Disks)

Editing newsletters, 162–163
Educational background of systems managers, 6

Electrical power:
    power management and diagnostic tools and, 248–249
    preventive maintenance and, 120–123
Electromagnetic interference, 173–174
Encryption to prevent unauthorized access to files, 112–113
Environment of machine, checking, 173–174
Etiquette for committees, 35–38
Executive training, 153–155
Experience of systems managers, 6–7
Expertise of systems managers, 42–43

Facts in newsletters, 162
FAX/MODEM communication tools, 244–245
Faxing, 205
Fear as reason for avoidance of spreadsheet use, 186
Fiber-optic cabling, 204
Files:
    backup (*see* Backup protection; Backups)
    backup (*see* Backups)
    deleted, restoring, 87
    naming conventions for, 183
    unneeded, 172
Floor layout, 58
    organizing and, 27
Floppy disks:
    backups of, 81, 88
    labeling, 171
    managing, 170–171
    virus protection and, 96–97, 105
Floppy-drive heads, cleaning, 120
Focus studies, 227–231
    examples of, 230
    goal statement for, 227–228
    information gathering for, 228–229
    option evaluation for, 229
    (*See also* Communications focus; Departmental focus study)
Follow-through, help desk and, 140
Follow-up:
    of departmental focus study, 198
    of source code audit, 130
Forms:
    application, for systems managers, 3–6
    application audit, 126, 127
    application inventory, 57, 58

Forms (*Cont.*):
    application revision request, 129
    backup procedures audit, 90
    call support, 142
    commercial software inventory, 56
    CPU inventory, 49–50, 52
    data loss, 84, 85
    departmental focus study overview, 193–194
    document analysis, 181
    hard drive audit, 175–176
    new/revised application notification, 84, 86
    new technology evaluation plan, 213
    new technology proposal, 212, 214
    preliminary functional analysis, 195
    preventive maintenance service report, 52–54, 118–119
    printer inventory, 51, 52
    restoration trial, 87
    service request, 33
    software copyright violation, 103, 104
    systems security analysis, 113–114
Fraud, 106
Full disk recovery, 89–92

Goals:
    action plans and, 21–22
    of committees, 41–42
    of disaster plan, 68
    of focus studies, 227–228
    mission statement and, 20–21
    organizing and, 27
    strategic planning and, 235
    (*See also* Objectives)
Grammar in newsletters, 162
Greed as reason for accessing files without authorization, 110

Hard-disk maintenance, 169–177
    audit procedures for (*see* Disk audits)
    conventions for, 169–171
Hard drive audit form, 175–176
Hard drives:
    backups of, 81
    organization of, 174
Hardware:
    disk, maintenance of, 120
    insurance coverage for, 72–73
    inventory of, 48–52
    strategic planning and, 235

Help desk, 135–144
  call management and, 140–143
  division of labor for, 136
  knowing when problem is solved and, 143–144
  objectives of, 135–137
  prioritizing calls and, 143
  skills and attitudes for, 137–140
Help desk review subcommittee, 39
Help desk tools, 245–246
Hierarchy of communication, 203
Hiring systems managers, 1–9

Improved performance as objective, 19
Improvement plans, strategic planning and, 236–241
Independent study, 150
Information gathering:
  for focus studies, 228–229
  for new technology review, 215
Information systems (IS) division, organizational position of, 13–17
Insurance coverage, 72–73
Insurance issues subcommittee, 38–39
Integrity, criticality analysis and, 64
Interviewing for systems managers, 3, 6–9
Inventory taking, 47–59
  of applications, 57–58
  of commercial software, 55–57
  of hardware, 48–52
  preventive maintenance checkups and, 52–54
  reasons for, 47
  recordkeeping for, 54–55
  schedule for, 55
  of skills, 48

Jargon:
  help desk and, 139–140
  in newsletters, 162
Job application form for systems managers, 3–6
Job elimination by new technologies, 217–218

Keys to commercial software, 56

Labeling:
  of backups, 81–84, 89
  of floppy disks, 171
Ladder of communication, 203

Leadership of meetings, 36–37
Legal audits, 99–107
  custom software and, 104–106
  forewarning users of, 101–102
  fraud and, 106
  initial, 101–103
  legal issues subcommittee and, 107
  party responsible for, 102–103
  piracy and, 99–101
  report of, 103–104
  service contracts and, 105–106
  unauthorized access and, 106–107
  viral infections and, 105
Legal issues subcommittee, 38, 107
Licenses of commercial software, 55
  software piracy and, 99–101
Line conditioners, 122
Listening skills of help-desk staff, 138–140
Logging:
  of backups, 31, 32, 80
  of database systems, 188
  of help-desk calls, 141
  of service requests, 28
  of significant events, 32, 33
Logic bombs, 94–95
Logs section of Master Planner binder, 28

Magazines read by systems managers, 7
Maintenance:
  of disk hardware, 120
  preventive (*see* Preventive maintenance)
Manufacturers (*see* Vendors)
Master Planner binder, 27–28
Media:
  for backups, 80–81
  failure of, restoration process and, 89
Meetings:
  for departmental focus study, initial, 192
  of word-processing users group, 158–159
  (*See also* Committees)
Memos:
  introducing departmental focus study, 192
  introducing executive coaching sessions, 154, 155
  introducing word-processing users group, 157–158

270 Index

Menu systems, standardizing on, 170
Microwave connections, 204
Milestones, 27–28
Mission statement, 20–21
   organizing and, 27
   strategic planning and, 235
Motives for unauthorized access to files, 109–111

Naming conventions for files, 183
Network management utilities, 246–248
New purchases, getting notification of, 54, 84, 86
New/revised application notification form, 84, 86
New technology evaluation plan form, 213
New technology proposal form, 212, 214
New technology review, 209–218
   elimination of jobs and, 217–218
   evaluation of technologies and, 212–214
   gathering information and, 215
   implementation and, 217
   new technology subcommittee and, 210–211
   product evaluation and selection and, 216–217
   proposals and, 211–212, 214
   responsibility for, 209–210
New technology subcommittee, 39, 210–211, 217
Newsletters, 161–166
   editing, 162–163
   publication schedule for, 164
   reader surveys and, 165
   reasons for, 161–162
   topics for, 163–164
Notification:
   of backup audits, 91
   of legal audits, 101–102
   of purchase of new applications and revisions, 54, 84, 86

Objectives, 18–19
   of help desk, 136–137
   (*See also* Goals)
Office layout, 58
   organizing and, 27
Open Items list, 27

Operating systems:
   experience with, 7
   standardizing on, 170
Organizational chart, 13–17
   organizing and, 26
Organizational goals, achieving, as objective, 19
Organizing, 25–34
   Master Planner binder and, 27–28
   project folder and, 28–31
   systems profile binder and, 26–27
   workstation folder and, 32–34
Orientation of new systems managers, 9
Outcomes, measurable, for action plans, 236

Pakistani brain virus, 95
Panel discussions, 150
Parking drives, 173
Passwords:
   for commercial software, 56
   to prevent unauthorized access to files, 111, 112
PC management tools, 243–254
Performance, improved, as objective, 19
Performance improvement:
   as objective, 19
   strategic planning and, 236–241
Performance-tuning tools, 174, 176
Philosophy of training, 145–146
Physical inventory (*see* Inventory taking)
Physical isolation for security, 111
Piracy, 99–101
Planning (*see* Action plans; Disaster planning; Planning committee; Strategic planning)
Planning Committee, 39–42
   communications subcommittee of, 39–40
   help desk review subcommittee of, 39
   new technology review subcommittee of, 39
   standards subcommittee of, 40
   (*See also* Strategic planning)
Plans section of Master Planner binder, 27
Political correctness of newsletters, 162
Power management and diagnostic tools, 248–249
Power supply, preventive maintenance for, 120–123
Preliminary functional analysis form, 195

Preventive maintenance, 117–124
  disk hardware maintenance and, 120
  external once-over in, 123–124
  first checkup for, 52–54
  internal tasks in, 117–120
  for power supply, 120–123
  purpose of, 117
Preventive maintenance service report form, 52–54, 118–119
Printer inventory form, 51, 52
Printer management tools, 249
Privacy, 106–107
Product list, 255–262
Product support of commercial software, 55
Programming experience of systems managers, 6–7
Project folder, 28–31
Proposals for new technologies, 211–212, 214
Protection:
  backup (*see* Backup audits; Backups)
  of data, Security Committee and, 38–39
  as objective, 18–19
  power supply and, 120–123
  for sensitive information, 106–107
  of source code, 79
  (*See also* Backup audit; Backups; Disaster planning; Security procedures; Virus protection; Viruses)
Purpose, mission statement and, 20–21

Qualifications for systems managers, 1–9

Radio frequency (RF) transmissions, protecting against, 120–122
Read/write path failure, restoration process and, 89
Readability of newsletters, 162
Reader surveys for newsletters, 165
Remote access tools, 249–250
Rental machines for restoration of disk, 91
Reporting software license violations, 100
Reports:
  of legal audits, 103–104
  preventive maintenance service, 52–54, 118–119
  year-end, 233–234

Resistance to departmental focus study, overcoming, 194
Restoration trial form, 87
Revenge as reason for accessing files without authorization, 111
Revisions of applications (*see* Application additions or revisions)
Rights, to custom software, 104–106
Roundtables, 150
Routine maintenance subcommittee, 39

Sags, protection against, 121, 122
Satellite connections, 204
Scanning, 205
Schedules:
  for backups, 81
  of committee meetings, 40–42
  for inventory taking, 55
  for newsletter publication, 164
  for preventive maintenance, 123
Secretarial training, 155–156
Security Committee, 38–39
  disaster planning subcommittee of, 38
  insurance issues subcommittee of, 38–39
  legal issues subcommittee of, 38
  routine maintenance subcommittee of, 39
  (*See also* Criticality ratings; Disaster planning)
Security committee, legal issues subcommittee of, 107
Security procedures:
  to prevent unauthorized access to files, 111–113
  standard, 115–116
Security systems, 250–251
Sensitivity ratings:
  access audit and, 114–116
  criticality analysis and, 64
Service contracts, 105–106
Service request forms, 33
Service request log, 28
Shareware, viruses and, 94
Significant events log, 32, 33
Skills for help desk, 137–140
Skills inventory, 48
Software:
  antiviral, 96, 97, 254
  applications (*see* Applications; Custom applications)

Software (*Cont.*):
  backup, 80
  commercial (*see* Commercial software)
  custom (*see* Custom software)
  dialback, to prevent unauthorized access to files, 111–112
  for document management, 184
  insurance coverage for, 73
  PC management tools, 243–254
  piracy of, 99–101
  strategic planning and, 235
  TSR [*see* Terminate and Stay Resident (TSR) programs]
  viruses and (*see* Virus protection; Viruses)
Software copyright violation form, 103, 104
Software distribution tools, 251–252
Software metering tools, 252–253
Software Publishers Association (SPA), software piracy and, 100–101
Source code, protection of, 79
Source code audits, 125–131
  backup security and, 128–129
  development tools and documentation and, 127–128
  input/output and testing methods for, 128
  locating custom applications and, 125–127
  modified commercial software and, 130–131
  purpose of, 125
  revision management and, 129–130
  security ratings and, 127
Speaking ability of help-desk staff, 139–140
Spelling in newsletters, 162
Spikes, protecting against, 120–122
Spreadsheets, 184–187
  for backup system analysis, 81
  checking, 187
  complex, 187
  database applications and, 188
  encouraging use of, 186
  large, 187
  locating applications needing to be introduced to, 185–186
Standardization, 169–171, 219–226
  advantages of, 219–220
  candidates for, 220, 222–223

Standardization (*Cont.*):
  disadvantages of, 220
  implementation of, 224–226
  justification for, 220–221
  reasons for, 219
  task force for, 221–222
  testing and research and, 223–224
Standards subcommittee, 40
Storage procedures for documents, 183
Strategic links, criticality analysis and, 64–65
Strategic planning, 233–241
  action plans and, 235–236
  budget and schedule and, 236
  improvement plans and, 236–241
  mission statement and, 235
  sample of, 234
  trickle-down, 235
  year-end reports for, 233–234
Subcommittees:
  communications, 39–40
    (*See also* Communications focus)
  disaster planning, 38–39
  help desk review, 39
  insurance issues, 38–39
  legal issues, 38–39, 107
  new technology, 39, 210–211, 217
  routine maintenance, 39
  standards, 40
  for training, 146
Subprojects, 31
Surge suppressors, 121–122
Surges, protecting against, 120–122
Surprise element:
  backup audits and, 91
  legal audits and, 101–102
Systems list for criticality analysis, 62
Systems managers:
  expertise of, 42–43
  hiring, 1–9
  job of, 18
  objectives for, 18–19
  proactive approach for, 20
  qualifications for, 1–9
Systems profile binder, 26–27
Systems security analysis, 113–115
Systems security analysis form, 113–114

T1 lines, 204
T3 lines, 204
Tape backups, 81

Task force for standardization, 221–222
Technical certifications of systems managers, 6
Technical skills of help-desk staff, 140
Technogeneralists for help desk, 140, 141
Technology:
　for wide area direct connection, 203–204
　(*See also* New technology review)
Terminate and Stay Resident (TSR) programs, 172
　standardizing on, 170
Test-bed approach for new technology implementation, 217
Testing, overcoming barriers to, 148
Time study analysis, 192–197
Timeliness, service contracts with outside vendors and, 105
Training, 145–151, 153–159
　of executives, 153–155
　formats for, 149–150
　overcoming barriers to learning and, 148–149
　philosophies of, 145–146
　secretarial, 155–156
　subcommittee for, 146
　of systems managers, 6
　training trainers and, 150–151
　triggers for, 147–148
　word-processing users group and, 156–159
Trickle-down planning, 235
Triggering events for training, 147–148
Trojan Horses, 94
Troubleshooting experience of systems managers, 7–8
TSRs [*see* Terminate and Stay Resident (TSR) programs]

Unauthorized access, 106–107
　audits for (*see* Access audits)
Unauthorized software (*see* Legal audit; Piracy)
Underwriters Laboratories (UL), 121

Uninterruptible battery systems (UBS), 122
Uninterruptible power source (UPS), 122, 123
　determining size for, 123
Unrecoverable files, backup protection of, 78
User comments, application revision and, 130
User groups, 150
Users groups, word-processing, 156–159

Vacuuming of inside of computer, 119
Vendors:
　list of, 255–262
　of new technologies, gathering information from, 215
　service contracts with, 105–106
　for wide area direct connection technologies, 204
Virus protection, 93–98
　defensive policies and procedures for, 95–96
　responding to attacks and, 96–98
　tools for, 96, 97, 254
Viruses:
　activation of, 96–97
　legal responsibility for, 105
　self-replication of, 93–94
　strains of, 94–95

Want ads for systems managers, 2–3
Weighting scheme for standardization, 221–222
Wide area direct connection alternatives, 203–204
Word-processing users group, 156–159
Workload management tools, 253
Workshops, 149
Workstation folder, 32–34
Worms, 94
Writing ability of help-desk staff, 139–140

Year-end reports, 233–234

ABOUT THE AUTHOR

Katherine H. Emery is a senior partner with S-O-F-T Industries Corporation, a computer management firm in Southington, Connecticut. She has a master's degree in computer science from Rensselaer Polytechnic Institute, and she graduated magna cum laude from The University of Connecticut, receiving a bachelor's degree in management. Before joining S-O-F-T Industries Corporation, Emery worked as a senior software specialist with Digital Equipment Corporation. She has written numerous articles which have appeared in computer magazines such as *PC Magazine, PC Computing,* and other industry-related publications.